C000075982

How TCS
Built an Industry
for India

How TCS
Built an Industry
for India

R. Gopalakrishnan
Tulsi Jayakumar

RUPA

Published by
Rupa Publications India Pvt. Ltd 2020
7/16, Ansari Road, Daryaganj
New Delhi 110002

Sales Centres:
Allahabad Bengaluru Chennai
Hyderabad Jaipur Kathmandu
Kolkata Mumbai

ISBN: 978-93-5333-854-1

Fifth impression 2022

10 9 8 7 6 5

Contents

Preface

This book, *How TCS Built an Industry for India*, is the first volume in the *Shapers of Business Institutions* series that probes the mindsets, behaviour and actions of 'Shapers of institutions.' This book, just as the others in the series, is neither academic nor an anecdotal 'new mantra' book. Management, we believe, is a performance art and not quite a science, and practitioners rarely write about their experiences. Only talented academics and top-class consultants dominate management writing. This series, then, positioned at the intersection of practice and theory, is based on the powerful idea of 'Experience before Theory.'

Indeed, this book, like others in this series, has been co-authored by an accomplished management practitioner and a serious academic, a combination that is a distinctive feature of these volumes. We have used our experience, in the form of our real-life observations on long-lasting and values-based companies, to posit certain hypotheses. We then ask: Can such hypotheses form the basis of a conceptual business model, which can be validated through field interviews? Such an intersection of practice and theory is what sets this series apart from other books on organizations/business leaders, which may have a preponderance of either practice or theory.

The theme of this series is the shaping of good companies into business institutions. Were we to use imagery to distinguish between institutions and companies, the former would be solid, long-lasting and structurally strong, metaphorically like Delhi's Red Fort; the latter, on the other hand, would resemble a modern, convenient and practical bungalow. However, bungalows may just survive, they may crumble, or they may evolve into forward-looking institutions, enduring over time and proving to be role models for others interested in converting their own bungalows into institutions. Whether the bungalow simply survives or becomes an institution depends on many factors, which will be explored in these books.

India, in 2019, has more than 5,000 listed companies, as per Bombay Stock Exchange (BSE) data.[1] How many of these companies can evolve into institutions? What does it take for such a mutation? Does it even matter if more companies are shaped into becoming institutions? The authors believe that yes, it does matter, and quite a lot. They believe that the growth of the economy and jobs in India crucially depends on India Inc. producing more and more business institutions, not just more good companies.

---

[1]'India: BSE: Number of Listed Companies: Economic Indicators: CEIC.' India | BSE: Number of Listed Companies | Economic Indicators, 1 November 2019, https://www.ceicdata.com/en/india/bombay-stock-exchange-number-of-listed-companies/bse-number-of-listed-companies.

ICONIC GEN-L INSTITUTIONS

Around mid-2018, a group of academics from Bhavan's SP Jain Institute of Management and Research (SPJIMR) debated ideas around this theme. There are centurion companies and corporate groups, which we refer to as Gen-C companies, which bear all the hallmarks of institutions. These Gen-C institutions bear storied brand names like Tata, Godrej, Birla, Bajaj and TVS—all founded about a hundred years ago and thriving to this day.

The current interest, however, lies in the search for Gen-L institutions, with L standing for liberalization. The idea is to identify those institutions that were born or shot into exemplary growth around the time of India's liberalization in 1991, or in the last half-century. Each of these companies should have a public image that is generally free of controversy, and should have been around long enough for the researchers to make a reasoned judgment. The founder or the leadership team should have shaped the group or company into a sustainable, values-based and high-performing institution. Another criterion important to the authors was that the Shaper be alive and speak on the subject personally. The books in the series are not commentaries on the Shapers; they are intended to be more about the institutions and the institutionalization of mindsets, behaviours and actions.

It is important to mention that the SPJIMR team did not intend to make judgements and comparisons as awards juries do. The team was merely trying to identify some institutions that met certain broad criteria and provided a basis for research as exemplars—there would surely be more exemplars, yet unidentified.

The process we followed was to identify potential Gen-L institutions, get a consensus on the list from the relevant faculty group, and then write to the Shapers, inviting their respective group or company's participation. One company declined, but six agreed to participate—after subjecting the author group to fair scrutiny.

Scouring through academic literature, the team jointly summarized papers on institution-building and formulated the SPJIMR Mindset-Behaviour-Action (MBA) Grid—the research model that appears at the conclusion of each narrative along with the research methodology and process. This was followed by desk research on the company and field interviews.

The book is arranged into a sequence of chapters that, hopefully, make it both instructive and inspirational, describing the genesis and nature of the industry in which the company operates, the background of the Shaper, the evolution of the company and its people, the MBA instituted by the Shaper, the impact of their transformative leadership, and important experiences, outcomes and lessons—besides key reader takeaways on the 'ways of the company and the Shaper'. This series is a joint project by two well-established Indian institutions—Bhavan's SPJIMR and Rupa Publications, India's oldest book publisher and distributor. The authors and publisher hope that the reader derives both inspiration and learning from the lessons showcased by the six institutions that are the subjects for this series.

This book is about Tata Consultancy Services (TCS) Ltd.,

India's multinational information technology (IT) service and consulting company. Its founding leader, F.C. Kohli, will be 96 years of age by the time this book is published, and the authors were privileged to be able to interview him on his early days in this institution. In an orderly fashion, he was succeeded by S. Ramadorai, during whose tenure the company scaled in an unimaginably efficient manner. There were two more CEO successions after Ramadorai. TCS is known for having invented the offshore delivery model for software, which served as an iconic exemplar to many IT services companies that followed. It is no wonder that both Kohli and Ramadorai are regarded as the true bricklayers and Shapers of TCS, and indeed the Indian software industry.

What did they do and under what circumstances? What are the lessons an aspiring Shaper could learn? The book concludes with the 'TCS Way', which summarizes these actions and inspirations.

Chapter 1

A Black Swan Event

Circa 1960. The world is divided. India is shackled.

Love, Peace, Equality and Freedom are the buzzwords in the world of the rich. A group of four young lads from Liverpool croons 'It's been a hard day's night' and 'All you need is love' to hysterical fans across the world, who declare the Beatles to be the 'Gods of Rock n Roll'. 'Flower Children' in the United States of America (USA) seek to achieve a new American Dream. On the other side of the globe, India, a young, independent nation having emerged from long years of subjugation, is shackled by chains of scarcity. As a polity deeply influenced by Soviet ideology, India has chosen planning as a means of economic development when confronted with a massive influx of refugees as a result of the Partition, huge food shortages and mounting inflation. Yet, it manages to achieve an average annual growth rate of only 3.6 per cent over the Five-Year Plan plan period (1951–56), leading its policymakers to declare industrialization as the goal within the framework of a socialist society.

In the world, meanwhile, the US—the richest nation in the world—contributes to 53 per cent of the total output of the bloc represented by the rich Organization of Economic Cooperation and Development (OECD) nations. Other OECD nations, though smaller, compensate by growing fast, at a pace unimaginable today. Thus, Japan grows at an annual average rate of 9.7 per cent, while Greece grows at 8.7 per cent over the period 1960–65. Ironically, the US grows at a relatively slower rate of 4.7 per cent per annum over the same period.[1] Among the 'Less Developed Countries' (LDCs) in Africa, Latin America and Asia, India contributes the maximum output, yet records only a 2.9 per cent rate of growth—half that of its doppelganger neighbour, Pakistan.[2]

In the second decade of its Independence, India's policymakers advocated huge imports through foreign loans as a means of industrialization that focussed on heavy and basic industries rather than consumer goods. But faced with drought, declining agricultural production and the resultant distress, India struggled to feed its large population. Agriculturally weak, dependent on the US and western nations for food imports, and missing the necessary foreign exchange to fulfil its multiple requirements, it became a land of prohibitions and restrictions—not only on liquor, but also rice and milk. People were exhorted to eat wheat or consume milkless sweets, in a desperate attempt to tackle the frequent famines.[3] Guest Control Orders in

---

[1]'India: BSE: Number of Listed Companies: Economic Indicators: CEIC.' India | BSE: Number of Listed Companies | Economic Indicators, 1 November 2019, https://www.ceicdata.com/en/india/bombay-stock-exchange-number-of-listed-companies/bse-number-of-listed-companies.

[2]India contributed 16.3% of overall LDC output, and yet grew at only 2.9% p.a. over 1960-65.

[3]Mihir Bose, '1960s: India's Changing Phase', *India Today*, 30 November 1999,

various states, in a country that frowned upon ostentation at that time, meant that you could feed no more than 50 people—even when you were hosting a wedding reception. Further, with four wars—one with China (1962) and three with Pakistan (1947, 1965 and 1971)—that drastically shrunk its forex reserves, the need of the hour in India (alongside agriculturalists) was a strong military that could protect her borders from warring neighbours. The youth were exhorted to finish a mandatory three-year spell with the National Cadet Corps (NCC) in order to be allowed to even sit for their graduation examinations.

AN AGE OF AUSTERITY

Scarred by scarcity and restrictions, Indians had little choice when it came to spending. The Hindustan Ambassador motor car—the poor man's car—had a waiting period of four years, which was nothing compared to the waiting period of 12 years for the Padmini Fiat—an automobile from the pre-1991 period. The primitive telecom infrastructure and the prohibitive costs of making a long-distance call meant that speaking to one's near and dear ones was an occasional, well-rationed event. In today's age of dual SIM cards and even the poorest owning mobile phones, it is difficult—nay impossible—to imagine a time when anyone possessing a landline was perceived to be someone with 'connections' and regarded as a one-eyed man in the Land of the Blind.

https://www.indiatoday.in/magazine/india-today-archives/story/20070702-indian-decade-of-dos-and-donts-1960s-748418-1999-11-30.

Televisions, too, were similarly restricted to seven cities in India.[4] The government decided what programmes should be watched by India's residents. The government-owned television channel, *Doordarshan*, only telecast programmes relating to agriculture, health and family planning, twice a day. It was much later—in 1982—that the fortunate few who owned televisions were treated to half an hour of contemporary Hindi film songs on the weekly programme, *Chitrahaar*.

It was in this constrictive time, in 1962, that the House of Tatas set up a separate computing division to service the data processing needs of all Tata Group companies. It was a bold and inexplicable move in a country like India at that time. It marked the birth of the Indian computing industry and no doubt qualifies—and justifiably so—as a Black Swan event like no other. The event took people by surprise, given the social context of the day, possessed extreme impact, and yet, now—in retrospect—is seen as very ordinary and predictable. As Nassim Nicholas Taleb, author of the book *The Black Swan* (2007),[5] states:

> What we call here a Black Swan event has three attributes. First, it is an outlier, as it lies outside the realm of regular expectations because nothing in the past can convincingly point to its possibility.

[4]Dey, Jhumpa. Television and Cultural Orientation Among Indian Urban Middle Class Women in Guwahati City of Assam. Thesis. Assam University, Assam, 2009. Shodhganga. Web. <https://shodhganga.inflibnet.ac.in/bitstream/10603/94199/7/07_chapter%202.pdf>

[5]Taleb, N. N. (2007). *The Black Swan: The impact of the highly improbable.* New York: Random House.

Second, it carries an extreme 'impact'. Third, in spite of its outlier status, human nature makes us concoct explanations for its occurrence after the fact, making it explainable and predictable in hindsight.

These triple features: rarity, extreme 'impact' and retrospective (not prospective) predictability signify a Black Swan event. Yet, a small number of Black Swans explain almost everything in our world, from the success of ideas and religions to the dynamics of historical events, to elements of our own personal lives.

While the event itself can be categorised as a Black Swan event, the perplexing question is—how and why, within such a volatile business environment, was such an institution created? What are the forces that prevented the organization—subjected to uncertainties, bureaucratic rigidities and the complexities of the business environment—from sinking into a deep morass and becoming yet another instance of a transactional organization, and instead enabled it to hold out as a beacon of hope for students and practitioners of leadership and organizational behaviour? Can a study of such forces yield lessons for organizations and corporate leaders of the future?

The central theme of these books is such forces taking the forms of individuals, who, in their roles as leaders, steered these organizations through difficult times and, in fact, performed the unique function of actually shaping these organizations into institutions.

HOUSE OF TATAS: INSPIRING INITIATIVE FOR NATION-BUILDING

Leading this Black Swan event that heralded the rise and rise of the Indian computing industry was an indigenous company set up by a Parsi, Jamsetji Nusserwanji Tata. The Tata Group's history is itself a testament to the 'Shaper' mindset that leads to the creation of institutions that endure over time. Jamsetji Tata was the firstborn in a family of Parsi priests in Navsari, a small town in Gujarat. He was the first member of the family to decide to break the mould and enter business. A liberal education in Bombay (now Mumbai) inspired in him a mindset that saw an opportunity in every space, was not afraid of taking the risks involved in entering completely unchartered waters, and most importantly, looked at business not as a means of personal profit, but as a means of raising India and its citizens out of poverty.

In 1868, long before India achieved its Independence, he at the age of 29, started a private trading company with a capital of ₹21,000. This laid the foundation of the Tata Group. Subsequently, he forayed into textiles to fulfil the need for economic growth, and later even into luxury hotels. In 1903, the Taj Mahal Palace Hotel[6] was set up by the Tatas with the ultimate aim of developing the city through access to foreign capital and technical expertise. He could clearly see that the existing hotels were few, poor in quality, unimaginative in their menu and inspired no

---

[6]Russi M. Lala (2017): *The Creation of Wealth: The Tatas from the 19th to the 21st Century*, Penguin Random House, UK Edition.

confidence in foreign visitors, who thought of India as a poor, wretched nation. With several outbreaks of bubonic plague in Bombay city, the rat-infested hotels would have struck terror in the bravest of hearts. Thus he took upon himself the onus of providing a clean and safe hotel that could attract European and American investors and technical experts alike.

He had his heart set on three dreams: building an iron and steel company, entering into hydroelectric power, and creating a world class institute that would train Indians in science. The audacity of having such dreams in pre-Independent India is unimaginable today. He iron and steel dream was sparked after a visit to Manchester. He realized that the Industrial Revolution that had transformed Britain and other Western nations could probably be replicated in India with the right infrastructure. However, this was easier said than done. Restrictive government policies were bad enough; the complexities of prospecting in barely accessible areas and sheer bad luck made matters worse. Further, entrepreneurs like he also had to contend with British scorn for natives' ambitions.

Sir Frederick Upcott, the chief commissioner of the Great Indian Peninsular Railway, had promised to 'eat every pound of steel rail [the Tatas] succeed in making.' Jamsetji died in 1904. However, his dream of an iron and steel plant was brought to fruition by his son Dorab Tata and his cousin R.D. Tata. The Tata Iron and Steel Company (TISCO) set up its first iron and steel plant in 1907 and the first steel ingot rolled out of the Tata plant in 1912, almost eight years after Jamsetji's death. The setting up of the Tata Hydroelectric Power Supply

Company in 1910 and that of the Indian Institute of Science (IISC) in 1911 further reinforced the notion and the power of 'Shapers', whose work lives on long beyond their lives, and who—through their dreams and aspirations—influence and inspire the deeds of the living.

By the time India entered its first decade after Independence, the Tata Group had diversified into a large number of industries including textiles, luxury hotels, consumer goods like edible oils, soaps and detergents, electricity, iron and steel, airlines, chemicals, locomotives and engineering products.[7] Its decision to enter these industries was in perfect alignment with Jamsetji's vision for India and the socio-economic context of the time. Even its decision to step into cosmetics manufacturing—an ostensibly misaligned diversification—appears perfectly rational when one unearths the reasons behind such a move.

Flashback to 1950. India, a young, independent nation that could not afford to spend precious foreign exchange on Western cosmetics, witnessed a ban on these imports in the Finance Minister's Union Budget Speech. In response, different groups of women went to Prime Minister Jawaharlal Nehru's house in the mornings, seeking intervention. They had a complaint: 'Our lives are already full of drudgery; please let us enjoy the one thing that makes us look and feel special,' they pleaded. Nehru's daughter, Indira, empathized with them as she felt that women had been denied their chance of 'Shringar' (beautification). One morning, when the prime minister was accosted by a group of such women,

---

[7]'TATA Group History Timeline.' *Timetoast*. https://www.timetoast.com/timelines/tata-group-history.

he asked M.O. Mathai, his secretary, 'Why can't someone manufacture this stuff in India?'

Mathai immediately called up the resident director of Tata in Delhi, K.A.D. Naoroji (Kish as he was called), to ask what the Tatas could do about this request. He goaded them, 'Can't the Tatas go into the cosmetics business and manufacture, in India, the whole range of stuff—everything that women need?' He further assured Kish all government support for this project.

Kish, in turn, sent a telex to JRD Tata—the eldest son of Sooni and R.D. Tata, and the chairman of the Tata Group—and communicated the prime minister's request. JRD assigned this project to Naval Tata, director-in-charge of the only consumer Tata company at the time—Tata Oil Mills Company (TOMCO). In time, the project was taken up by Naval Tata's wife, Simone Tata. Lakmé was born![8]

In the 1960s, India was an economic disaster. It followed a path of development that focused on public-sector-led heavy and basic industries and had neither the willingness nor the ability to enter into highly capital-intensive, foreign exchange-dependent and skill-intensive technology such as that embodied in computers. It therefore remains a riddle as to how and why, within this chaotic social context, JRD thought of entering the super modern, technology-intense world of computers. Perhaps the senior leadership—especially Colonel Leslie Sawhney, brother-in-law, aide and confidante of JRD—had seen the manually noted records

[8]Mathai, M.O. (1979), *My Days with Nehru*, New Delhi: Vikas Publishing House, p. 47-48, retrieved from: http://www.enddynasty.com/wp-content/uploads/2019/02/2015.120866.My-Days-With-Nehru.pdf

being used in a conglomerate like the Tata Group, requiring large volumes of paper, and had advised JRD to centralize the data processing function into a single unit.

BIRTH OF TCS

Be that as it may, in 1962, on the advice of Colonel Sawhney, JRD decided to set up a separate division of Tata Sons that would service all data processing needs of all the Tata Group companies under one roof. Set up with a meagre investment of ₹50 lakh ($110,000), the unit office was located in Ballard Estate in South Mumbai. The unit, comprised 20 senior executives from various Tata Group companies—especially from the Tata Administrative Service—was in an unenviable position from the start. It was nobody's baby. It had no name; it was simply referred to as a division of Tata Sons; many of the staff continued to be on the payrolls of different Tata companies. It enjoyed no 'demand', as most Tata companies preferred to carry out their prime data processing activities in-house. It also had supply-side constraints in terms of non-availability of computers for carrying out data processing.

In 1964, computers were scarce in India and the only hardware choice that existed was between IBM (International Business Machines) and ICL (International Computers Ltd.). With some Tata companies already working with IBM machines, the new unit was predisposed towards IBM. However, at this stage, the team bought time from an IBM data centre to use their IBM 1401 computer. Such a lease was enough for the unit's initial work, which comprised relatively low-level share accounting and registry work that was deemed cumbersome by other Tata Group companies and involved the hassle of legal clearances as well.

By 1968, the unit had moved deeper into this business. It had leased two more IBM 1401 and purchased one ICL 1903, and built its reputation for share accounting and registry work on these leased data processing machines. It had even started eating into the market share of IBM's data centres, which provided similar data processing services. Owing to the Tata name, the organization and its leaders were able to attract some of the best young minds, educated in the top universities and educational institutes of the time both nationally and internationally. Despite its initial lack of sophisticated work, this talent was attracted early enough to impact TCS' ability to withstand and, in fact, challenge the competition.

An early recruit in 1965 was Lalit Kanodia—a young MBA graduate from the Massachusetts Institute of Technology (MIT), on a summer vacation in India before commencing his journey towards a doctorate from MIT. While in India, Kanodia met and fell in love with Asha, his future wife. It was love at first sight and Kanodia was determined to waste no time in getting married to his lady love. He had already proposed to her and she had accepted. However, the stars seemed to conspire against this young love. The pundits, unable to find an astrologically auspicious time, ruled out the possibility of marriage in the next few months. Determined to proceed to the US with his bride in tow, Kanodia requested MIT to defer his doctorate journey by one semester—long enough for an auspicious time to emerge. MIT acceded to his request. But Kanodia was not used to simply waiting with nothing much to do, especially during the day. Bored, he approached his neighbour, H. Ramanath Rao—an employee at Tata Fison—for some productive work with the Tata Group. One thing led to another, and he was introduced to P.M. Agarwala, the managing director of Tata Electric Company (now called Tata Power), who employed Kanodia. His first assignment was to write some papers on what Tata could do related to computers.

Kanodia wrote three papers, each of which contained a recommendation for the Tata Group. The first paper related to the automation of the Electric Companies' Load Despatch System; the second was on computerization of their billing system, for which he suggested buying computer time from Tata Institute of Fundamental Research (TIFR), which had a CDC 3600 at that time. However, Kanodia's third paper was the most interesting and contained the blue-print for starting a new enterprise, which was called the Tata Computer Centre.

Kanodia was married in November 1965 and returned to MIT in 1966, accompanied by his young wife. His status in the Tata Group was still that of an employee on leave without pay. In his absence, Agarwala, together with other Tata directors, accepted all of Kanodia's recommendations. They ordered a Westinghouse Computer to automate the load despatch of the Tata Electric Companies. They computerized their electricity billing and decided to set up the Tata Computer Centre.

Agarwala would often travel to the US and made it a point to visit Kanodia during these visits. He urged Kanodia to return to India and start the Tata Computer Centre for them. Kanodia was happy in the US and in no mood to return. Finally, Agarwala made him an offer he found difficult to refuse—he offered Kanodia the opportunity to head the new enterprise. Kanodia returned to India together with his two Indian colleagues from MIT, Nitin Patel and Ashok Malhotra. They established the Tata Computer Centre in 1967 as part of Tata Services Limited. In 1968, following the restructuring of the Tatas, this enterprise was renamed Tata Consultancy Services (TCS) and became part of Tata Sons.[9] Besides Kanodia and his colleagues, Patel and Malhotra, TCS, since its infancy, boasted of people with strong quantitative aptitude such as Praveen Gandhi and Yash Sahni. The only other company that had a presence in the computer and software industry at the time was Hinditron, founded in 1966 by Hemant Sonawala, who used to work for DEC in the US[10] and had returned to sell their equipment in India.

Kanodia worked with TCS until 1969 and subsequently established the Datamatics Group of Companies in 1975— which went on to become India's third significant company in the computer and software space.

However, the earliest 'Shaper' of the institution that we know today as TCS was a young technocrat, Faqir Chand Kohli, who joined TCS as general manager in 1969. The

---

[9]Lalit S. Kanodia, 'The software journey of India and the way going forward,' September 11, 2012, https://www.iaccindia.com/userfiles/files/ THE%20SOFTWARE%20JOURNEY%20OF%20INDIA%20AND%20THE%20 ROAD%20GOING%20FORWARD-%20By%20Dr_%20Lalit%20S_%20 Kanodia.pdf. Kanodia worked with TCS between 1968 and 1969, before he went on to establish the Datamatics Group of Companies.

[10]Digital Equipment Corporation (DEC) , also known as Digital—a large American company—was a leading vendor of computer systems, including computers, software and peripherals in the period 1960s-1990s. In 1998, it was acquired by Compaq.

induction of Kohli into TCS can itself be termed a Black Swan event. A power engineer turned accidental—and reluctant—data processing engineer, FCK, as he is popularly known, went on to become the chief architect of the institution that, in 2019, is the biggest job creator in the US.

At this stage it would be appropriate to pay tribute to another legendary person, Nani Palkhivala, who was the chairman of TCS in its formative years and played an important role in shaping the organization and Kohli. We spoke to our Shapers, as well as others connected with the era, to draw on the important contribution of this legal giant.

Kohli spoke with love and deep respect for what Palkhivala meant, both for TCS and to him. He said that Palkhivala gave him the freedom to run the company and supported him on all policy issues. Kohli's successor, Ramadorai, also spoke of Palkhivala as someone who was known for his brilliance and humility. 'Just by observing him, one could learn a lot. He was a person of impeccable integrity and one who allowed you full freedom to express your views. He valued time management and stayed focussed on issues at hand besides always being respectful of others and their capabilities. Having travelled with him to the US at least once a year, I could observe him keenly,' said Ramadorai.

Ramadorai also shared a small personal anecdote. 'Headed for Washington, Palkhivala and Kohli came by Concorde from London to New York City. They had to wait for a couple of hours at New York's La Guardia airport for a connecting flight to Washington DC. Kohli took the long journey in his stride. But having convinced the chairman to fly Concorde, Kohli gave me the task of managing Palkhivala. I looked at it as an opportunity for some exclusive learning time with him. As a professional, I observed how Palkhivala conducted himself and respected everyone irrespective of their status.'

Syamal Gupta, ex-director, Tata Sons, also remembered Palkhivala as a brilliant mind with a keen grasp of issues and seemingly unrelated matters. A simple and generous man, Palkhivala believed in treating everyone equally and not throwing his weight around. Gupta states, 'Palkhivala was the brightest star on India's legal firmament. His speech, an analysis of the Indian budget, drew crowds at the Brabourne Stadium, Mumbai, to the tune of lakhs of people who occupied the stands and the ground, which was a record in itself. To be blessed with a brilliant mind and to use it for the good of society with far-reaching implications, and yet remain grounded and modest, was perhaps the biggest lesson that Palkhivala taught all of us.'

One of the authors of this book, R. Gopalakrishnan, former director, Tata Sons, spoke of the statesmanlike role played by Palkhivala with regard to TCS' initial forays into the US market, which is remembered fondly by all associated with the era. Palkhivala used his network of contacts to introduce TCS to potential clients and guided the company on what was legal and what was not. He provided the strong connect between JRD and TCS, and gave Kohli the courage to try the unknown through his support.

The duo of Kohli and Ramadorai played a key role in preparing TCS for a Black Swan event like no other witnessed in the twentieth century. Here was a company from India, a developing country, undertaking a reverse voyage in search not of great riches but of lands that offered greater opportunities for the development of IT given the unfavourable conditions at home. The fascinating journey of this institution and the man shaping it—much like the early sea voyages of explorer-navigator Christopher Columbus—provided the springboard for other companies to follow, and transformed India into a global IT hub.

Chapter 2

Kohli Discovers a 'New World'

By prevailing over all obstacles and distractions, one
may unfailingly arrive at his chosen goal or destination.

—Christopher Columbus

The story of the birth of TCS under Kohli in the twentieth
century reminds one of the first-ever expedition to
America, led by the Italian explorer Christopher Columbus
in the early sixteenth century. Both events were accidents
of history, rather than products of a grand design; both led,
metaphorically speaking, to the discovery of 'new worlds';
both resulted in huge transformations, leading history to
immortalize one as the most famous explorer that the world
has ever known, and the other as the 'Father of the Indian
IT industry.'

Columbus, son of a wool merchant, was born in Italy in
an era when the lure of vast riches and undiscovered lands
was great. He worked aboard a merchant ship as a teenager,
which sparked his fascination with the sea. Desirous of

discovering India—known for its riches—he was convinced that it lay across the Atlantic. He finally found someone to back his ideas in 1491. The monarchs Ferdinand of Aragon and Isabella of Castile signed a contract with Columbus, in which they promised him 10 per cent of all the riches he found and the governorship of all lands he encountered. Finally, in his fourth voyage, he 'discovered' America instead of India, which he had set out to discover. His discovery led to a complete transformation in the lives of the natives through the conquest and colonization that it unleashed.

Similarly, the son of a textile merchant, born on 28 February 1924 in Peshawar in undivided India, acted on his conviction that India could become the global IT hub by creating and exporting value rather than just trying to sell software services within the country. He was F.C. Kohli, and he created a new industry in India and helped explore unchartered territories.

TCS bears testimony to the latent Indian never-say-die entrepreneurial spirit and its ability to find ways and means to survive under the most difficult conditions. Its journey to becoming one of the top three global software services companies in 2019 is the story of a seafarer's voyage in search of elusive lands.

Kohli completed his college education at Government College, Lahore—known as one of the oldest seats of learning in the Muslim world. After completing his BA (Hons) in English, Kohli went on to acquire an additional bachelor's degree in applied mathematics and physics. That year, the Government of India announced a scholarship for young students desirous of pursuing higher education in the US. Kohli wished to change his profession to engineering. He applied for the government scholarship and won it.

Kohli went to Canada in 1946 to pursue his engineering education. He left behind a prosperous family in Peshawar, who owned one of the largest textile trading companies at the time. He topped his class and received a bachelor's degree in electrical engineering from Queen's University in Kingston, Ontario, Canada in 1948. He then worked with Canadian General Electric for a year. With his savings, he wished to pursue his master's from the MIT. However, MIT waived the fees and Kohli successfully earned a master's degree in electrical engineering in 1951. Although he received several job offers in the US, Kohli wanted to pursue a PhD at MIT. But first he wanted to meet his family, as he had not seen them in five long years. He had been unable to travel earlier as flights between India and the US were extremely expensive and infrequent back then, and a ship would took 31 days to make the journey.

In the meantime, his family—affected by the Partition of India—had been forced to leave Peshawar. They had migrated and settled down in Lucknow. Their textile trading business was now a mere shadow of its former self. So, when Kohli returned home in 1951, he was shocked to see his once prosperous family sleeping on the floor and almost in a state of penury.

Kohli says, with a catch in his voice, 'I was shocked when I saw them. And to think my brother had sent me $1500 when I was in the US. How did he manage it? I cried all night and decided not to return to the US.' He looked for a job as he resolved to try and restore the lost glory that his family had enjoyed until recently.

On a side note, one wonders what would have happened had the Partition, a Black Swan event in its own right, not occurred, with its deep and wide-ranging impact, scattering and displacing millions of people across two countries—India and Pakistan. Would India still have had the 'Bhishma Pitamah of the Indian IT industry' to lead it? Would the IT industry have enjoyed one of its biggest evangelists?

CHARTING A NEW ROUTE

Kohli received a job offer from Tata Electric and joined the company in 1951. He spent nearly two decades there, during which he is credited with designing a system that has delivered stable, high quality, uninterrupted electricity to the city of Mumbai till date, rivalling New York. In 1963, he wrote a paper, 'Economics of long-distance extra-high-voltage transmission lines', which won great acclaim and provided the plan framework for setting up the Power Grid Corporation of India. In the mid-1960s, under his leadership, Tata Electric was the third utility company in the world and the first in Asia to employ a digital computer to plan load despatch.

In 1968, Tata Sons, with a view to enhancing their income, decided to restructure some of their units as operating divisions. Four separate divisions were established—Tata Consulting Engineers, Tata Economic Consulting Services, Tata Financial Services and TCS. The Tata Computer Centre became part of TCS, with Agarwala, the managing director of Tata Electric, being appointed as the director of TCS in addition to his other responsibilities. One reason for choosing Agarwala could have been that Tata Electric was possibly the only Tata company that had given the fledgling data-processing unit started by JRD, sophisticated work at a time when most other Tata companies continued to handle their data processing in-house.

Agarwala worked closely with Kohli, who by then, had risen to become the deputy general manager at Tata Electric. He knew that Kohli possessed the intellectual acumen to run the new unit. Moreover, Kohli's knowledge of computers was unrivalled at the time. He decided to ask Kohli to join TCS. There was only one glitch: Kohli had no interest in moving out of Tata Electric. He dreamt of heading Tata Electric someday, and a move to TCS would mess up this ambitious plan. But Agarwala persisted. He specifically created a post of general manager for Kohli, and finally persuaded the latter to join, albeit reluctantly.

The new environment required a new set of skills, and Kohli would spend hours poring over technical manuals at home to acquaint himself with the technology. He could see that getting to the top by providing data processing services would be a long and arduous process. But he perceived a possible short cut, much in the same way that Columbus perceived a shorter route to the 'Indies.'

While a leader always gathers a strong working knowledge of the technical environment that he is managing, a Shaper is one who not only gains sufficient knowledge of the technical environment, but is able to see the gaps and shape the environment to suit the growing capabilities of the organization.

TCS was originally positioned as a data processing unit. But there weren't many takers for such services—neither in the government, nor in the private sector. Kohli gauged this anomaly and decided to take the route of 'Management Consulting'. As a consultant, TCS would scout for clients to whom they would offer management consulting. Once a client buy-in had been established and the clients felt engaged, TCS would recommend automation and electronic data processing (EDP) work as a means to a more efficient management. It was a roundabout way to succeed in an era where data processing and computing were virtually unknown. But it worked!

TCS was able to attract several well-recognized and reputed organizations, including Hindustan Aeronautics Ltd. (HAL), Delhi Development Authority (DDA), and the Department of Atomic Energy (DAE) of the Government of India. The work done for these clients helped build TCS' reputation, and it was able to establish itself as a thought leader in this space. By the 1970s, however, the internal demand became insufficient to sustain the group.

Meanwhile, the nationalization of private banks in India, which commenced in 1969, increased the need for computerization. TCS was involved in this task. As the first round of nationalization was completed by 1971-72, Kohli had simultaneously covered the entire backlog of computerization within India's banking system. However, the government did not want any more computers in India, as it believed computers would lead to mass unemployment. Kohli was bored and saw no future for himself in computers.

He was fascinated with the application of electronics and data to power transmission and hence had engaged with computer companies to install the load despatch system in Mumbai. A load despatch system is the *sine qua non* of a modern, urban setting, as it is the nerve centre for the operation, planning, monitoring and control of the power system required for the efficient functioning of urban centres.

For Kohli, moving to TCS was a one-off dabble in computers. Now, with the computerization of nationalized banks completed and no other opportunity in sight, he yearned to return to the power sector. He went up to JRD and expressed this desire to go back to Tata Electric. Even as JRD tried to convince him to stick with TCS and give it a go in EDP, two events occurred that helped to retain Kohli in TCS and shape the development of the institution.

The first event occurred in 1972–73, when Kohli was elected as a director of the Institution of Electric and Electronics Engineers (IEEE) (Region 10) in New York—in fact, the first Indian to be nominated for this prestigious position. He was aware of TCS' dependence on IBM computers and wished to mitigate it. In his capacity as director, IEEE, Kohli often visited the US. He made eight trips to the US that year, during which he developed contacts and close relationships with senior managers of the US computer manufacturer Burroughs Corp, the second largest computer company in the world.

Around the same time, another unexpected event happened. In 1974, Agarwala, who had fallen ill, began to work from home, but succumbed to his illness a few months later. Kohli was immediately appointed director-in-charge and was required to directly report to the TCS Consultancy Committee, comprised of Tata Sons Directors A.B. Billimoria, Freddie Mehta and Nani Palkhivala. The idea of working with these stalwarts and influencing and shaping a new company in an emerging field was probably a key factor that made Kohli stop insisting on going back to Tata Electric. Automation and computerization held growing business potential, and this was a leadership opportunity like no other. Kohli decided to stay with TCS and build it to become the global IT giant that it is today, in spite of the politico-economic climate in the country.

BIRTH OF INDIAN SOFTWARE

As described earlier, India was in a politico-economic quagmire during the 1960s and much of the 1970s, with a high degree of economic controls on the private sector—which was almost considered a necessary evil and shackled by multiple licence requirements. With four wars and shrinking forex reserves, the government promoted an 'extreme inward orientation', with industry required to produce all that it could within the country, irrespective of the cost, so that things would not need to be imported.[11] In fact, a combination of high import duties (the highest in the world), highly regulated interest rates and a prohibition of Foreign Direct Investment (FDI) stifled industrial growth.[12]

Harish Mehta, founder of NASSCOM, recalls the tough

---

[11]Ajit Singh, 'The past, present and future of industrial policy in India: Adapting to the changing domestic and international environment,' Working Paper no. 376, Centre for Business Research, University of Cambridge, https://www.cbr.cam.ac.uk/fileadmin/user_upload/centre-for-business-research/downloads/working-papers/wp376.pdf.

[12]Chetan Ghate, Stephen Wright and Tatiana FC, 'India's Growth Turnaround,' in *Oxford Concise Companion to Economics*, p. 33-40, https://www.isid.ac.in/~cghate/Concise_OUP_GWF.pdf.

business environment in India during the 1970s, which was unconducive for computers—which were practically non-existent. As an electrical engineer from Pune with a Masters in Computer Hardware in the US, Mehta had returned to pursue career opportunities in India. After applying to three companies, including TCS, he joined Hinditron. 'Skills were absent. There were hardly a few people in Mumbai who were database experts—about 10,' he says.

Hard infrastructure was a greater issue than soft infrastructure. Today, we are so accustomed to computers and the Internet that we do not appreciate the critical role that telecommunications, especially telecom infrastructure, has to play in their efficient functioning in a manner that can enable offshoring.[13] The growth of offshoring of IT-enabled services is linked to the availability of large amounts of reliable and affordable communication infrastructure, especially telecom pipes, used to transmit large amounts of complex data over long distances almost instantaneously. However, in the India of the 1970s, there was no telecom facility and data had to be physically and manually transferred.

One of Hinditron's first few clients was Vulcan Laval based in Pune.[14] Speaking about the way business was done in those days, Mehta explains how they would collect all the company data on punch cards once a month, bring it to Mumbai, transfer it to a tape and bring the tape to Hinditron.

---

[13]Off-shoring refers to the practice of basing a business or a part of the business in a different country on account of favourable tax considerations or lower costs.

[14]Vulcan Laval's name was changed to Alfa Laval in 1987. Alfa Laval is a heavy industry company that focuses on large-scale operations, such as the marine, energy, and food industries.

They would then process it, print the results and then send it all back to Pune. 'What you call cloud computing today, we did it in a medieval way,' he chuckles.[15]

Electricity was another major issue. The Vulcan Laval work required eight hours of consistent power supply. If the power went out in the seventh hour, they would have to start all over. 'I used to watch movies in Eros Cinema, when there were power failures. I ended up watching the same movie so many times. What could you do?' he says with a shrug of his shoulders. Voltage fluctuations were also common despite the use of voltage stabilizers and inverters. A battery back-up lasted 20 minutes, which was really inadequate given the erratic nature of power supply.

Then there were the foreign exchange and other regulations by the Reserve Bank of India (RBI). 'When we imported computers, for example, there was no hedging. We borrowed ₹13 lakh from ICICI for the import. By the time we repaid, we had paid ₹26 lakh besides interest. There was no cover,' he reminisces. The business also meant investing heavily in spare parts inventories, because given the import restrictions, they could not afford breakdown of their most expensive equipment for too long.

The telecom pipes were also subject to regulation. 'We could do the offshoring job at one tenth of the cost in India and export through the telecom pipes. Without the telecom

---

[15]To understand the early days of computers and Internet in India, one may refer to: Srinivasan Ramani, 'The story of how the Internet came to India: An Insider's account,' *News 18*, 14 August 2015, https://www.news18.com/news/tech/the-story-of-how-the-internet-came-to-india-an-insiders-account-1039533.html.

pipes, how do you export, how do you do offshore work?'
he says, adding, 'There were hundreds of such regulations
in India at the time.'

The Tata Group, the parent company, in keeping with the
times, had the bulk of its sales coming from heavy industry—
raw materials, energy and chemicals. But, it was within this
tough business environment, characterized by economic
misery, that Kohli led TCS into the first world—which, in
turn, led to the birth of the Indian software industry.

A SHAPER EYES THE FIRST WORLD

Kohli's contact with Burroughs during his visits to the US
opened his eyes to the vast potential that computers held for
India. He began to envisage a partnership with Burroughs,
partly as a means of mitigating the dependence on IBM, but
also as a way to get India to embark on a computer revolution.

Kohli's move to enter into a joint venture (JV) with
Burroughs allowed TCS to import and distribute Burroughs
computers. Burroughs, too, was driven to the JV because
of the strict Foreign Exchange Regulation Act (FERA)
restrictions in India, under which the government had
imposed strict regulations on cross-border payments as well
as transactions that could affect the country's meagre forex
reserves. A foreign multinational could operate in India
only through a JV with a domestic firm; further, foreign
ownership was restricted to a maximum of 40 per cent.
Thus, while Burroughs needed a partner who could help
deal with the bureaucratic procedures involved in entering
and running a business in India at the time, TCS needed

this partnership to gain access to new technology.

Kohli ultimately wished to use such access to manufacture computers in India itself. Burroughs had also agreed to sell them a B1728 'small system' computer that was expected to help TCS facilitate training of its engineers to programme and write software applications, which could be used to develop software and sell software services in foreign markets. This, in turn, could help TCS earn the foreign exchange to buy more computers.

However, the stringent import restrictions on the private sector meant that TCS received permission to import the computer only after committing to export twice its import value over the next five years. The entire process of importing the computer, with the requirement of clearances at both ends—from the Indian government as well as the US defence department—was time consuming, taking between nine months and a year. To access foreign exchange to pay for the import, TCS then had to borrow in rupees and convert the loan into foreign exchange—all of which worked out to be much costlier. TCS finally managed to import the computer only in 1974. The B1728 cost them $340,000. However, due to the exchange rate volatility, TCS ended up paying twice the amount on account of the import duty. Worse, exemplifying the unpredictable policy changes, just the day after TCS managed to import the Burroughs mainframe computer, the finance budget announced a dramatic reduction in the import duty on computers from 101.25 per cent to 60 per cent.

The export commitment attached to this import meant that TCS, per force, had to look outside to drive its business. It was the beginning of the Indian outsourcing model. TCS perfected the art of carrying out part of the development work in India, and then sending its programmers to the US or other foreign locations to install system software and help clients migrate software running on IBM and other systems on to its own hardware platforms.

TCS thus began to take up outsourcing contracts for Burroughs. The very first contract involved converting a hospital accounting package called the Burroughs Hospital Information System (BHIS), written in Burroughs medium systems COBOL, to Burroughs small systems COBOL. An unused ICL 1903 machine acquired from a Calcutta (now Kolkata) Life Insurance Corporation (LIC) branch at a fraction of its purchase price was used to write the assembly program. The communist trade unions of LIC had blocked the use of this machine over the threat of loss of jobs, and the machine sat in its covers, unopened. While it suited TCS to buy this machine off LIC and made eminent economic sense, this was a manifestation of the business challenges that faced computer manufacturers in India. The Indian mindset was against automation and computerization, which were seen as Western tools to substitute human labour with machines.

Thus, it was not surprising that when Tata Sons finally received the licence to manufacture Burroughs equipment in India in 1977, they decided against entering the computer manufacturing business. The risks of such business in India were perceived to be very high. Even IBM exited India in 1977, citing concerns regarding protection of its intellectual property based on dilution of equity.

However, in 1978, Tata Sons, formed a formal JV with

Burroughs called Tata-Burroughs that sold and maintained Burroughs computers in India. The new company put TCS, then barely ten years old, into a challenging and awkward situation. It had two choices: either it could choose to be enfolded into the Tata-Burroughs entity, or it could continue to exist independently. In the latter case, however, it would have to seek and bag non-Burroughs business, and in doing so, would have to compete with Tata-Burroughs. It was a tense period between TCS and Tata Sons. Kohli, however, stuck to his belief that TCS should continue as a separate entity.

We believe that it was at this point that Kohli really started exhibiting the traits of a Shaper, as enunciated in our Shaper's MBA grid. Gone was the reluctant CEO of TCS, who had gone and requested JRD to send him back to Tata Electric! The 'Critical Thinking' mindset, so characteristic of Shapers, was clearly visible here—a mindset that considers options and their pros and cons through mental evaluation. Kohli understood the challenge that he faced by working in a Burroughs-dominated environment; and yet, he knew that TCS would need to start from scratch, if need be, and work almost as a start-up, just to not succumb to the temptation of being merged with Tata-Burroughs. At the same time, a Shaper's mindset evaluates the short-term and the long-term carefully. While short-term considerations may have dictated TCS to merge with Tata-Burroughs, Kohli knew that was not what long-term interests demanded.

Finally, Minoo Modi, the chief executive of Tata Sons, blinked; he allowed Kohli to have his way, with the understanding, however, that TCS would transfer twenty-five of its key people to Tata-Burroughs. This was again a tough clause, as most employees would have preferred the relative safety afforded by the Tata name—especially when combined with the formidable multinational, Burroughs. How could Kohli prevent some of his best brains from seeking sanctuary in the known and the comfortable?

Again, we see another crucial Shaper mindset, that of 'People Relations', coming into play. Shivanand Kanavi, the well-known technology journalist who was then vice-president, TCS, has known Kohli for two decades and describes him as a 'man of very few but carefully chosen words.'[16] Although known as a man who spoke little and who did not suffer fools gladly, he had the ability to impact people around him enough to heed his clarion call.

For instance, when Jayant Pendharkar and S. Ramadorai—people who went on to occupy key roles at TCS as Head of Global Marketing, and CEO and MD respectively—were offered positions in Tata-Burroughs and Kohli requested them to stay back, there was no question of their choosing the safety and security of a well-established multinational organization over the relative insecurity and obscurity of a start-up. Both Pendharkar and Ramadorai chose to remain at TCS.

An 'Orbit Changing' mindset was again demonstrated by Kohli even as he chose to break the umbilical cord with Burroughs. The Indian domestic market was not ready for computers in the way that the West was, and Kohli felt that

---

[16]"TCS@50: Why India Must Be in Eternal Debt to F C Kohli.' *Rediff*, Rediff.com, 31 Mar. 2018, https://www.rediff.com/business/special/tcs50-why-india-must-be-in-eternal-debt-to-f-c-kohli/20180331.htm.

rather than struggle to compete in India, it would be better to focus outside India. This leads us to another important Shaper instinct—namely, the recognition that 'Every problem has an opportunity hidden in its womb.' Kohli could see the opportunities that lay at the end of the long tunnel if they could remain unfazed by the challenges of the prevailing business environment and political climate in India at the time. Quite unlike the then political masters, who couldn't envisage the shape of things beyond 30 years, Kohli knew that with science, a long-term view is critical.

Kohli's out-of-the-box thinking made TCS the first Indian software and services company to obtain permission to set up an overseas unit in New York. Leading this journey into the first world was Subramaniam Ramadorai, Kohli's peerless soldier. When Ramadorai was sent to New York in 1979, his mandate as the first TCS resident manager was to build a new revenue stream for TCS from IT software and services. Thus began the journey of a group of Indians in search of elusive markets that would allow them to conquer the 'First World' and transform a small Indian IT start-up into a global IT giant. India had come full circle![17]

What was it about Ramadorai that made Kohli root for him and choose him even when the former had no sales background? Sales and marketing were critical to the new independent entity. Yet, Kohli had built his opinion of Ramadorai through his multiple interactions with him. He

---

[17]Krishnan, Raghu. 'Computers Must Start Speaking Regional Languages: FC Kohli, First CEO of TCS', *Economic Times*, 1 May 2018, https://economictimes.indiatimes.com/tech/ites/computers-must-start-speaking-regional-languages-fc-kohli-first-ceo-of-tcs/articleshow/63982038.cms;

felt there was no one else whom he could trust more—a faith that re-emerged when he had to anoint his successor, almost 17 years later.

By then, three decades since its inception, TCS had more than 90 per cent of its business outside India. With a revenue of $160 million, it employed 8,000 employees. TCS, under Kohli, had ridden against all obstacles to make its entry into the First World. It had no choice but to be a 'global' company when it was time for a change of guard. The formidable Kohli anointed his successor CEO, the unassuming Ramadorai (or Ram as he was popularly known),[18] in 1996.

---

[18]We will use Ramadorai and Ram interchangeably throughout the book.

Chapter 3

Ramadorai Rides the Millennium Wave

Teamwork is the ability to work together towards a common vision. The ability to direct individual accomplishments toward organizational objectives. It is the fuel that allows common people to attain uncommon results.

—Andrew Carnegie, Industrialist

When Ram took charge of TCS in 1996, the world that he faced was completely different from the one faced by Kohli in 1968. Computers had become a mainstay and an intricate part of all businesses around the world, with both private sector companies and governments crucially dependent on them for their operations. However, a big problem lurked in the near future.

The year 2000 was anticipated to bring a major computer bug that threatened to affect all computer code developed for mainframe computers since the 1960s. The root cause of the problem, likely to occur on 1 January 2000, was that computer engineers had written complicated computer programmes through the 1960s to the 1980s using a two-digit code rather than a four-digit code to represent the year. In other words, the year 1999, say, would be written as '99', with the first two digits being left out. This had been done with a view to saving valuable memory space. However, at the stroke of midnight on 31 December 1999, the dates would change to 1/1/00, rendering it difficult for computers to interpret the date as 1 January 2000 and not 1 January 1900. All calculations based on the date would then fail, leading to chaos.

Christened by global IT pundits as the Y2K bug, this tidal wave threatened to engulf all leading economies critically dependent on computers and computer systems. Healthcare systems, power plants, transport systems, banks and financial institutions were all likely to be badly hit by the 'millennium bug', as also the fortunes of companies like TCS. At the same time, there were other competitors, younger and more nimble-footed, who threatened to claw away market share as well as public perception. Could Ram, the shy and reticent trainee who had joined the company in 1972 and emerged as the 'chosen' one, ride the Y2K wave to success for TCS and also complete its transformation into an 'institution'?

As we see it, the transformation of the institution is so closely interwoven with the personal metamorphosis of the Shaper that the distance between the Shaper and the institution gets blurred; the Shaper becomes an institution and the institution becomes a Shaper. This is probably nowhere as clear as in the case of Ramadorai and TCS. Thus, an understanding of the creation of the modern-day TCS is to be viewed through the lens of the metamorphosis of Ram.

EARLY YEARS: FOLLOWING THE HEART

Ram was born on 6 October 1945 in Nagpur in a traditional Tamil Brahmin family that greatly underscored the importance of academics—especially mathematics, arts and music. However, Ram was not particularly fascinated by academics in his early days of schooling in Delhi, much of which he attributes to the Indian education system. A timid child, he never understood the tendency of Indian teachers to shower their attention on only the brightest students in the classroom, thus contributing further to a feeling of inadequacy among the not-so-bright ones.

Young Ram had few friends in school and books were his constant companion. He had inherited his love for reading from his parents, who were both voracious readers. And while his love-hate relationship with academics took a turn for the better when he entered college and ranked amongst the top three in his class, he continued to remain shy and always scared of being picked on by the teacher—even when he knew the answers.

Ram's father had pinned his hopes on him to fulfil the former's dream of having one of his five children become a doctor. However, the road to doing so started with dissecting a frog preserved in odorous chloroform, which Ram found heart-wrenching. An unexpected surge of courage compelled him to tell his father that it wasn't to be—he could not study medicine! In retrospect, of course, this loss for the medicinal world was a gain for the fledgling Indian IT software industry.

Ram enrolled for a bachelor's degree in Physics and Mathematics at Hansraj College, an institution established in 1948 by the D.A.V. Managing Committee—initially only for men[19]—and located in Delhi University's North Campus. The college boasts of illustrious alumni in diverse fields such as films (Shah Rukh Khan, Anurag Kashyap, Tarsem Singh), politics (Kiren Rijiju, Vijay Kumar Malhotra), journalism (Vinod Dua) and industry (Naveen Jindal). By now, the academic bug had bitten Ram, who next enrolled for a degree in Electronics and Telecommunications at the (IISc), Bangalore, from where he graduated in 1968—the year TCS was established. A short stint at the Physical Research Laboratories, Ahmedabad, made him desirous of pursuing a doctorate. Thus, in 1969, Ram found himself headed to the University of California at Los Angeles (UCLA) with a full scholarship to pursue a course in computer science at the master's level.

While it is common to see members of the Tamil Brahmin community settled in the US today, Ram was the first member of his family to get an American education. Naturally, his family—especially his mother—was apprehensive about his well-being. They were also concerned about losing their child forever, as it was not common for Indians studying abroad to return to their country. This phenomenon, known as 'Brain Drain', is as true today as it was 50 years ago. Further, given Ram's temperament, his mother's heart was concerned about how her shy young boy, brought up on vegetarian food and

---

[19]In 1978, the college became co-educational. One of the authors of this book also graduated from Hansraj college more than two decades later.

with few friends in India, could manage and survive in a strange land with meat-eating, English-speaking strangers.

However, Ram found the atmosphere in the US exhilarating and strangely liberating. While he was worried about living up to his family's expectations, Ram found the academic culture in the US very unlike India. 'Students were encouraged to ask questions, irrespective of their ethnic backgrounds or even academic credentials. This gave me confidence,' he says. Living in Los Angeles also made him more self-reliant, working as he was, because he now had to be responsible for his own lodging fees, cooking, and keeping house all at the same time.

After completing his Master's at UCLA, Ram decided to stay back and take up a lucrative job offer that came his way from National Cash Register (NCR) in Hawthorne, a Los Angeles suburb. The job's starting offer of $12,000 per annum, along with the promise of a bright future ahead in the flourishing US computer industry, was a dream come true—one which other young computer graduates, especially Indians, would have given an arm and a leg for.

In the meantime, Ram's mother informed him of Mahalaxmi (Mala), a pretty young girl they had considered as his prospective bride. Of course, she insisted, the 'decision' to marry was ultimately Ram's. As is the practice among Tamil Brahmin families entering into 'arranged' marriages, the prospective groom, accompanied by his family, would visit the girl's house for what was traditionally called 'Ponnu Pakkal'—the bride 'seeing' ceremony. Following this ritual, Ram's family and Ram himself were keen on the match. However, Mala insisted that she would agree to the wedding only after Ram returned from the US and found a job in India. Considering her age at the time—19 (to Ram's 26)— and the fact that she was entering an arranged marriage, where traditionally the groom's family called the shots, this was rather bold and unconventional.

Ram was thus faced with a difficult choice, involving a tussle between his head and his heart. As he stated in an interview: 'In a corner of my heart my strong nationalistic upbringing kept tugging at the option of coming back to India.'[20] Then there were his parents, as also his to-be-wife, who finally helped him make up his mind to return to the country.

As Ram puts it with disarming candour, 'Most times I have been lucky when I have listened to my heart.' He did not mind Mala's reluctance in agreeing to a US-based groom; in fact he decided to write to her once he got back to India and took up a job with TCS, to allay some of her fears. The letters did the trick! Mala must have revised her initial opinion of Ram as being too conservative and orthodox, given that she herself came from a fairly liberal and well-off family. She consented to the marriage and they were married in 1972.

A Shaper understands life's challenges and the critical choices that are to be made. He has the ability of critical thinking—evaluating the pros and cons of each option and

---

[20]S. Ramadorai, 'Five experiences that shaped the life of S. Ramadorai, Vice Chairman, TCS,' *Economic Times*, 28 March 2014, https://economictimes.indiatimes.com/five-experiences-that-shaped-the-life-of-s-ramadorai-vice-chairman-tcs/articleshow/32789340.cms?from=mdr.

Between 1996 and 2009, TCS grew from a $160 million firm to a $6-billion behemoth. https://www.thehindubusinessline.com/info-tech/Ramadorai-retires-from-Tata-companies/article20881769.ece

then making informed choices based on a mental evaluation of these options (and possible alternatives).

TAKING RISKS: LEARNING BY DOING

When Ram traded a $12,000 per annum US pay packet for a $1,600 per annum Indian one with TCS and domestic bliss, he became aware of the deep similarities between a corporate career and kite flying—a sport which had defined his childhood and given him cause for much celebration in his younger days. Pongal, the harvest festival for South Indian celebrated in the month of January, was an occasion for kite flying, a popular sport in India. As a child, Ram was fascinated by kites. The risk involved in pitting one's kite against another, the anticipation, the thrill, and the excitement when a rival's kite was cut even as one's own continued to soar in the sky, was something that gave him an adrenaline rush like no other. As a child, he would also be wonderstruck by how a kite always flies against the wind, never with it.

Moving back from the US was a professional risk. As he states, 'Risk-taking was to become a recurrent theme in my life.' After joining TCS in March 1972 as an assistant systems programmer and analyst, his first test came when Kohli asked him to stay back in TCS during the split between TCS and Tata-Burroughs. The choice was between a start-up in a hostile environment and the ease of a multinational organization, but one which might stifle freedom and flexibility and the potential to grow. What made the choice particularly difficult was that the Burroughs-less entity had no real experience in sales and marketing, a function hitherto led by Burroughs.

Moreover, the markets that they would have to build were unknown foreign markets, as the Tata-Burroughs deal had forced upon TCS a non-compete clause in Indian markets.

As Ram made up his mind to follow his heart and stay back with Kohli to build TCS, he was asked to proceed to New York as TCS' first resident manager. And thus, in 1979, Ram went back to the US—wife and son in tow—to build a new revenue stream for TCS.

What was it about Ram that made him believe that he could survive and build a business for TCS in a country where India was seen as a land of snake charmers, incapable of selling anything other than mysticism (and definitely not software services)? Being a hardware person, how could he adapt to performing a sales role, for which he had no background? Ram modestly puts it down to the 'brash confidence' that accompanies youth. However, we see such confidence and risk-taking ability as the early signs of a Shaper mindset. It is a mindset that allows a Shaper to clear obstacles and break barriers in dogged pursuit of the goal.

What is visible from these early days is Ram's Shaper mindset, which believes in 'Learning by Doing'. As Ram states, 'I was a one-man start-up, so apart from making cold calls to potential customers, I typed letters, sent faxes and sometimes I was even the delivery boy. No job was menial for me.'

It helped little that his boss in New York, Naval Mody, president of Tata Inc.—the US subsidiary of Tata Sons—saw little value in Ram's presence and role there, given that he had no faith in sales as a concept and considered trading to be sufficient. Survival in the US while leading a one-man army was, at this stage, more about grit and determination than just talent in building a new business in foreign lands.

Two years of hard work led to breakthroughs with IBM, Tandem, Hewlett Packard (HP) and other hardware vendors, further setting the stage for larger projects and opportunities. It was tough work, but Ram persisted. He believed that TCS was not just building a new business, but a new industry for India.

Typically, organizational decisions are made on the basis of cost-benefit analyses; a similar sense of personal costs vs benefits or risks vs rewards governs decisions and efforts expended by individuals on a particular task or activity. However, we sense that Shapers tend to also consider the costs and benefits to the nation in organizational or even personal decisions—enough for such national considerations to tip the balance. We noted this in the multiple conversations we had with various people regarding both the Shapers considered in this volume; the sense of 'nation' superseded everything else.

A 'HUDDLE GROUP' FACES THE Y2K BUG

Ram had worked in multiple roles at TCS and taken on many challenges, moving from hardware to software, from sales to marketing and so on. As the time for a leadership transition at TCS approached, it was left to Kohli to decide whom to pass on the baton to. The choice was between Ram, who headed the US operations, and Dr Nirmal Jain, the head of the European operations. Despite a clear difference in Ram's personality from his own, Kohli chose him as the successor.

He probably realized that TCS, in its next growth phase, would require a leader who was more people and client-oriented than himself—qualities that Ram possessed in good measure.

Ram was clear that he could never emulate Kohli's leadership style, which was strong, bold and visionary, but was based on the concept of 'one leader'—almost autocratic. Kohli's mentoring style was also firm and critical, so that people would learn. Ram was certain that while such a leadership style had its place under the sun in the initial stages of TCS, while it was being built from scratch, the next phase needed a different approach. He wanted to build a more participatory culture and a collegiate team atmosphere with a policy of active inclusion, where all opinions would be solicited and all voices would be heard. Even as Y2K approached, he realized that the new wave would have to be ridden by a leadership *'group'* rather than a *leader*.

And thus it came about that much before the Indian cricket team popularized the 'huddle' in 2003 as it marched towards the finals of the ICC Cricket World Cup, Ram formed his very own strategy 'huddle group'. The core group comprised S. Mahalingam (Finance), N. Chandrasekaran, S. Padmanabhan (HR), Ananth Krishnan (Chief Technology Officer) and Ravi Viswanathan (head of TCS operations in Chennai). In addition, the huddle group also comprised academics like Pankaj Ghemawat from the Harvard Business School. The group would meet at least once a week at Ram's home at Worli Seaface in Mumbai, usually on a Saturday or a Sunday. Such meetings encouraged frank and free sharing of ideas, with no hierarchies and officious strings attached. After Ghemawat joined them, the nomenclature of the meetings changed, and the core group came to be known as the corporate 'Think Tank.' However, the collegiate management style envisaged under the concept of the 'huddle group' continued; a deep bond developed among the members of the think tank, which, as Ram attests, had its own advantages and uses—especially in meetings with clients. The closeness meant that each of them knew exactly what the others were thinking merely by reading their body language or tone of voice. In such leadership styles, we witness the 'people's relations' aspect of the Shaper MBA Grid, with a mindset that is respectful of others and values people's relations over all other criteria, and translates this into actions that are empathetic to others.

Such a leadership style enables Shapers to take challenges in their stride and overcome them better. This was amply evident in the handling of the Y2K crisis—one of the major and earliest challenges Ram faced as the CEO and MD of TCS. The Y2K bug was both a software and a hardware problem, involving the electronic programmes that were used to tell the computer what it must do as well as the machinery of the computer itself. As countries like US and Australia spent billions of dollars, Indian companies, led by TCS, were at the forefront providing 'Y2K compliant' programmes. India itself offered a large, untapped pool of low-cost labour—an advantage missing in Western countries, leading to a burgeoning Indian IT industry in the wake of the Y2K problem.

Where TCS scored above its competitors was in their 'first-mover advantage', enabled by a visionary leader—a Shaper. Firstly, as part of its original business, TCS possessed indigenously developed migration tools that helped it import a huge number of programmes and lines of code into the TCS systems, correct the date references, test them and then finally ship the corrected code to the customer. Secondly, TCS established a software factory in Chennai, where most of its mainframe capabilities lay, as the Y2K was essentially a mainframe-oriented problem. Thus, TCS was able to handle about 600-700 million lines of code and increase its revenues from $125 million in 1995 (the year before Ram took charge) to $419 million in 1999, even as it maintained its operating margins at 32 per cent.[21]

'ONE TCS'

As the company expanded, Ram felt overwhelmed by the sheer scale of the business—which had now spread to about 20-25 countries across the world. So far, TCS had been operating as a start-up where people would do their own thing, performing multiple functions and creating applications required for these functions using disparate technologies, based on need. There were no Enterprise Resource Planning (ERP) systems in place. Ram, upon enquiry, found that there were actually more than 1,200 applications running inside TCS, developed by different departments and business units to fit their own needs. However, even as TCS braced itself for Y2K and planned growth, it was clear that such duplication of systems made little sense; it made moving data between

---

[21]'Y2K Bug,' *National Geographic*, https://www.nationalgeographic.org/encyclopedia/Y2K-bug/; Ramadorai, S (2011). *The TCS Story... And Beyond*, New Delhi: Penguin.

these units next to impossible, given that it would lead to loss of accuracy, integrity and timeliness.

Ironically, while TCS was emerging as a reliable solution provider, building extremely sophisticated integrated systems for its clients (including stock exchanges and banks), its own systems were 'archaic and non-integrated'. TCS needed an orbit change; it needed to embrace technology to create a single unified system—'One TCS'.

A team approach led to the development of a unified information system called e-TCS, which would help support the organization's anticipated exponential growth. However, the best of ideas fail if they are not accepted by users; and herein lies the challenge of all Change Management. Internal marketing usually happens to be far more difficult than external marketing and branding. Getting the buy-in of the majority stakeholder group was critical to influence behaviour, and in this case such stakeholders meant TCS employees themselves.

Ram appointed a chief transformation officer (CTO) for the task—a first for any Indian software company. Paighal S. Viswanathan, the CTO, had a background in not only technology, but also sales and marketing. One of Vishwanathan's first initiatives was to rebrand the e-TCS package as 'ULTIMATIX', which was an acronym for 'the ultimate system.' Further, rather than 'nudge' people into using the system in phases in a piecemeal fashion, he felt that it had to be an 'all-or-nothing' option—rolled out to adopt a 'big bang' approach and get everyone to switch at the same time.

The Ultimatix was a high-risk affair, requiring a $40 million investment in technology that could, after everything, still fail.

Keep in mind that at the time, overall company revenues were about $700 million. The project had to be ratified by the Tata Group Business Review Council for the sheer quantum of investment it required. Ram backed the project all the way. The company intranet was finally launched on 1 April 2002. It was a system that enabled TCS to bring together data about projects, clients, employees, prospects and even customer relationships under one portal and made the vision of 'One TCS' come true. It has since been upgraded in keeping with TCS' business needs, and represents the backbone of TCS business processes today.

LEADING A TRANSFORMATION

Even as the Y2K problem provided the platform for growth, the corporate think tank at TCS was being pushed to dream big—set a vision for the future that would look audacious, but successfully propel TCS into the league of the top global IT companies in the new millennium. In 2003, TCS derived 90 per cent of its revenues from IT services. A brainstorming session led to the conviction that TCS would need to expand not just the market share but also the range of services offered. Five additional areas were identified for TCS to grow its business in: Global Consulting, Engineering and Industrial Services, Asset-Based Offerings, Infrastructure Services and IT-enabled Services (or BPO).

The question that arose was: what would be a good target goal to achieve? Should growth be envisioned in terms of the traditional metrics of revenue and profits, or was it a better idea to simply aim for a global position? The group decided that they would aim to be among the top 10 IT software and services company by 2010. TCS revenues at this time were about $1 billion.

The goal was already daring and bold when along came the tsunami of the 2008 Global Financial Crisis to make it even more difficult to achieve this Big, Hairy, Audacious Goal (BHAG). However, it was achieved—albeit three years later than intended, in 2013, when TCS displaced Montreal-based IT services firm CGI to rise to the tenth spot both in terms of revenue and market share. Its other Indian competitors— Cognizant, Infosys, Wipro and HCL—were placed at the fifteenth, eighteenth, twentieth and twenty-fifth positions respectively (See Table 1: Joining the Top League in 2013).[22] What was remarkable and beautiful, however, was that TCS' profit margins were way ahead of others on the list, at 28.4 per cent. IBM, the top IT company, came in at 17.9 per cent.

Table 1
2013: JOINING THE TOP LEAGUE IN 2013

Rank 2013	Service Provider	Estimated 2013 Revenue* ($BN)	Market Share (%)	Profit Margin (%)
1	IBM	54.4	8.6	17.9
2	Fujitsu	32.1	5.1	5.9
3	HP	29.2	4.6	2.8
4	Accenture	25.4	4.0	15.3
5	NTT	16.7	2.6	4.7

---

[22]Shilpa Phadnis, 'TCS Joins Top 10 Global IT services Companies Club,' *Gadgets Now*, 22 April 2014, https://www.gadgetsnow.com/tech-news/TCS-joins-top-10-global-IT-services-companies-club/articleshow/34067479.cms.

6	SAP	15.4	2.4	NA
7	Oracle	13.5	2.1	NA
8	Capgemini	13.4	2.1	8.3
9	CSC	12.4	2.0	8.9
10	TCS	10.5	1.7	28.4
15	Cognizant	7.7	1.2	19.0
18	Infosys	6.0	0.9	23.5
20	Wipro	4.7	0.7	21.3
25	HCL	3.9	0.6	22.2

*Revenues are for the calendar year 2013 and only for IT services. Excluded are BPOs, R&D services, Software/Hard ware products.

TCS' rise to the top 10 was driven by its aggressive targeting of renewals and new business, particularly in continental Europe. Its hallmark, as remarked by analysts, was the flexibility in its pricing and terms and a reputation for winning any deal anywhere in the world at any price it wanted. Further, it had emerged as a viable alternative to the tier-1 companies—the top IT companies at the time, mostly from the West, such as Accenture, IBM, CSC, Capgemini or BearingPoint—all of whom baulked at taking on low-margin, low-value work. It had also developed a reputation for coming in and fixing messy contracts and implementations.[23]

What kind of a Shaper mindset could result in such a remarkable achievement? We would attribute it to the twin values of frugality and groundedness possessed by Shapers. Typically, high profit margins are difficult to achieve in conjunction with high revenue growth. Thus, while TCS

---

[23]Ibid.

grew its revenues, it kept a sharp eye on costs. Again, a manifestation of its groundedness was the fact that no job was considered low enough to be rejected, even when TCS aspired to be among the Top 10. But to reach this position, it had to move out from under the canopy of Tata Sons and test its market value by literally going public.

MARKETING BLITZKRIEG FOR $1 BILLION IPO

Imagine you are the CEO of a pioneer company, which has several firsts to its credit:

- It is the first software and services company in India (1968).
- It is the first Indian software company to set up operations in the US (1973).
- It is the first Indian company to conceptualize and develop the network offshore delivery model.
- It is the first company to set up a software and process engineering research centre (1981).
- It is the first to establish a Global Delivery Centre (2001).
- It is the first Indian software and service company to cross the magic $1 billion (₹45 billion) revenue mark (2002-03).

However, ironically enough, you are the best kept secret of India's IT industry! Worse, your competitors are credited (mistakenly) for all these firsts. This could mean one of two things: Either you head an extremely publicity-shy, reticent group that lets its actions speak for itself; or your competitors are loud, market-savvy, and good at PR. Worse still, it could mean both! That, unfortunately, was the case with TCS right up to 2003.

As Ram puts it, 'There was a visible perception amongst the investment community, for instance, that Infosys was the company of the future and that TCS was living in the past. The media would portray and report the same.'

It was also the year before a historic restructuring of Tata Sons would lead to TCS floating an IPO to become an independent public company. The restructuring itself was an extremely sensitive topic, and had taken almost five years. At stake were the cash flows that Tata Sons would lose in return for the amount that would be realized through an IPO. In 2002, TCS became India's first billion-dollar company. It now made sense for Tata to dilute its stake and thus an 'in-principle' decision was taken to launch the TCS IPO in May 2004.

For TCS, the IPO was crucial for various reasons: First, it had to compete with Wipro and Infosys, both of which were listed. The process of listing, it was felt, had contributed significantly to the competitors' brand value. Hence, it was necessary for TCS to also take the route of public listing. Secondly, post the IPO, TCS could reap the benefits of similar public attention and PR coverage; third, the IPO would facilitate TCS in offering stock options as a means of retaining and nurturing talent among its employees; fourth, the resultant size and stature derived from the IPO would help TCS compete with global majors for mega-million dollar projects; fifth, it would provide TCS sufficient financial muscle to achieve its vision of becoming a global company.

As authors M.G. Parameswaran and Kinjal Medh have noted in their book: 'The TCS IPO was a critical move for the company; it was, in a sense, a coming-of-age moment that would significantly transform the company in the eyes of all its stakeholders—employees, customers, prospects, media, regulators, prospective employees and the government.'[24]

As per Securities and Exchange Board of India (SEBI) guidelines, companies could not advertise in the period leading up to an IPO, defined as up to three months before an IPO. Companies could, however, undertake pre-IPO advertising before the prospectus was filed and approved by SEBI, comprising typically of big corporate image advertising that described key financial details such as turnover, profits, etc.

Ram had no doubt that the TCS IPO would be over-subscribed within just a few hours, given that the pricing was 'expected to leave something on the table' for the small investor. He was aware that his company's persona was similar to his own persona of yore—publicity-shy and reticent. Therefore, the question was: Now that the 'beautiful girl' was ready to 'unveil herself' (words used to describe TCS by Ishaat Hussain—finance director of Tata Sons—after the TCS road show prior to the IPO), how to establish her stature on dimensions that the financial community and other target audiences were unaware of?

Given TCS' numerous firsts on the global arena, the core creative campaign that Ram approved was based on the idea of 'TCS—Truly Global'. It was a four-ad-campaign devised by

---

[24]M.G. Parameswaran and Kinjal Medh (2011), *Draft FCB+Ulka: Brand Building Advertising, Concepts and Cases*, 2011, Tata McGraw Hill Education.

FCBUlka, comprising full-page colour newspaper ads, which sought to present TCS as an Indian company that was global in its scale, operation, ethos and ambitions. The four ads had four specific areas of focus. The headlines of these ads were as follows:

1. 'IT put India on the world map. But who put IT on the Indian map?' (TCS pioneered the Indian IT software and services industry).
2. 'When does the day end when you're working around the clock, round the world?' (TCS pioneered the global delivery model).
3. 'Money makes the world go round. But who makes the money go round?' (TCS has core strengths in the financial services IT software segment and more).
4. 'Do you ever think of software saving lives?' (TCS is investing in research in this critical area of importance).

Each of these advertisements also carried the basic bio-data of TCS—the six core areas of its functioning, viz. Consulting; IT services; Engineering and Industrial services; Asset Based Solutions; BPO; and IT Infrastructure; as well as its size and scale. For the first time, it became public that TCS was a company with 149 sales offices in 32 countries. It had over 28,000 employees of 30 nationalities, six clients out of the US Fortune Top 10, and Global Development Centres in 17 cities across nine countries outside India. With strong client relationships and constant investment in R&D, it had the ability to scale the breadth and depth of technology capability and deliver large scale system integration projects globally. The organization had strong people management policies and the lowest attrition rate—6.1 per cent—compared to other tech majors. These aspects of the company were highlighted in its pre-issue advertisements, and termed as the 'Seven Wonders.'[25] The four-ad campaign was signed off with the tag line 'Truly Global.'

The campaign, which ran in leading Indian English newspapers, financial newspapers and magazines as well in international magazines like *The Economist* and *Time*, boldly proclaimed that TCS had arrived on the centre stage and was the future. The campaign, however, lasted for just about three weeks till the SEBI approvals came through for the IPO; however, it was successful in presenting to its various stakeholder groups a holistic view of TCS' pioneering past, its global-level competencies and its vision for the future.

The IPO, however, had to be postponed from its initial launch planned in May 2004 due to the prevailing political scenario, which affected stock markets negatively. TCS finally made its IPO offering in July 2004. The biggest single IPO in Indian corporate history comprised an IPO offering of 55.5 million shares of face value ₹1 each, through a book-building process with a bid price of ₹775-900 per share. The issue price of TCS shares was fixed at ₹850 per share, making it the first billion dollar IPO in Indian history, raising ₹54 billion ($1.2 billion).

TCS received bids for 91 per cent of the shares on offer on the first day itself. The issue closed with an over-subscription of 7.7 times. On listing, the stock opened at ₹1198.97,

---

[25]'Mr S Ramadorai, CEO, Tata Consultancy Services.' *www.indiainfoline. com*, https://www.indiainfoline.com/article/news-sector-others/mr-s-ramadorai-ceo-tata-consultancy-services-113111400164_1.html.

commanding a 41 per cent premium on the issue price. TCS shares were listed on both the National Stock Exchange (NSE) and the BSE on 25 August 2004 at a premium of 26.6 per cent, at ₹1,076.

The IPO enhanced TCS global image, transforming it from a division of an unlisted public company to an independent enterprise with its own corporate identity. The vision for implementing this exercise lay with the Shaper, Ramadorai, who integrated people, policies and processes to lead this transformation.

BRANDING TCS: EXPERIENCE CERTAINTY

While the pre-issue advertising pushed TCS into the limelight, the company still had no strategic branding to boast of. Its competitors, despite their late entrant status, had been able to create the perception of being market leaders in the Indian IT industry; TCS suffered relative anonymity despite being the pioneer of the Indian IT industry and its business models. This not only affected clients, but also its ability to recruit the best talent.

Most Indian IT companies pitched themselves generically by touting the 'India advantage' of being companies with low-cost manpower but sound software engineering skills. While this pitch was successful, leading to revenue growth of 30 per cent and profits growth of 20-25 per cent for the industry,[26] it was unsuccessful in distinguishing

---

[26]Shishir Prasad, 'TCS takes first steps for global IT brand', *Economic Times*, 19 March 2007, https://economictimes.indiatimes.com/tech/software/tcs-takes-first-step-for-global-it-brand/articleshow/1776352.cms?from=mdr.

one Indian company from another. Indian companies were seen as cheap and efficient service providers, but the more challenging and complex assignments still went to Western tier-1 companies. The latter were perceived to be more reliable business partners.

Ram's conviction that the world would be dominated by only the three top IT companies made it necessary to undertake strategic branding to distinguish TCS from other competitors. This was a clear move away from his mentor, Kohli, who had little belief in branding and advertising. TCS' branding agency Siegel & Gale's research indicated that apart from IBM and Accenture, no other IT services company occupied a clear position in the IT buyer's mind. With IBM positioning itself on innovation and Accenture on business performance, it was felt that TCS' most believable claim would be how solid its software was. With more than 50 per cent of software products likely to be defective, reliability in software delivery was the top gap area and what most IT directors really desired.

TCS' strength in this regard was reaffirmed by an incident that Siegel & Gale Group Director, Denis Riney, experienced and narrated: 'I was at a global IT conference where I met an IBM Global Services person. He said TCS had better people, better product, but luckily (for IBM) they did not know how to market themselves.'[27]

The 'Experience Certainty' campaign was born in 2007. It was simple enough to mean something for everyone at TCS. For instance, as Ram put it, 'What I liked about the

---

[27]Ibid.

tagline "Experience Certainty" was that it was something to live up to at any time and all the time. If a consumer or a prospect came to India for the first time, I would like the TCS chauffeur to feel inspired to be there on time to receive him, wearing a starched white uniform and driving a nice clean car. We wanted to ensure that "Experience Certainty" started from the smallest detail, and extended all the way up to the top.'[28]

The Shaper mindset of 'stakeholder orientation'—i.e. an orientation which aims at benefitting all parties affected by the future success or failure of an organization (stakeholders), and not merely its shareholders—ensured that 'Experience Certainty' was not merely a marketing slogan or gimmick. The TCS executive team, led by Ram, had ensured a substantial budget for internal training of the workforce. It was important for the campaign to actually lead to a difference that personnel at all levels in the company—including front line sales and delivery personnel—could perceive in their day-to-day interactions with clients. Simultaneously, it was important to reinforce internal commitments involving issues such as day-to-day collaboration on project teams and divisional financial targets. It is such attention to customer and community perspectives that sets Shapers apart from leaders.

FOUR DECADES OF EXCELLENCE

Kohli (1968–1996) had set the ball rolling for India's IT sector by building TCS as a global company. Between 1996 and

---

[28]S. Ramadorai, *TCS Story*, p. 163.

2009, Ram not only transformed the company from a $160 million firm to a $6 billion behemoth, but also changed the culture of the organization from one based on a single leader to one based on a participatory model of idea sharing. TCS was firmly riding the wave of success. Between the two, Kohli and Ramadorai ensured 41 years of excellence—an excellence that had the ability to sustain itself for long thereafter and to shape TCS from an organization into an institution.

In the next chapter we shall explore the Shapers' mindset-behaviour-action, which helped turn TCS into the institution that we know today.

Chapter 4

Shaping Excellence
into the Company DNA

Excellence is never an accident. It is always the result of
high intention, sincere effort, and intelligent execution; it
represents the wise choice of many alternatives—choice,
not chance, determines your destiny.

—Aristotle

The rise of the IT industry in India and its pioneer torch-
bearer, TCS, were Black Swan events—rare, extremely
impactful and, in retrospect, highly predictable. How much
were these events influenced by the two individuals who were
responsible for the TCS journey over 41 long years? It would
not be an exaggeration to state that such Black Swan events
were indeed shaped by these individuals, who rose from
being *leaders* leading their organizations, to *Shapers*—who
not only shaped the destiny of their organizations, but that
of the very nation.

However, rather than looking at Kohli and Ramadorai

separately and gleaning aspects of their mindsets and actions as those of Shapers, we shall do the reverse. We shall look at those mindsets and actions that can be attributed to 'Shapers' in general, and unearth instances of such mindsets, behaviours and actions in Kohli and Ramadorai. In doing so, it will become amply clear why such mindsets, behaviours and actions are key to the development of an institution—be it building leaders for posterity or even being influenced by a nation-centric mindset.

Organizations, to remain sustainable, need a pool of talent that can envision and implement change in perpetuity. An important characteristic of Shapers, thus, is their ability to identify and attract great talent and subsequently develop a sequence of leaders for eternity. Thus, the process itself can be seen as a sequence of four inter-related steps: identifying talent, attracting it, nurturing it and retaining it.

While attracting and retaining talent in any industry is a difficult task, the computer industry in India presented its own peculiar challenges. In fact, Thomas Watson, founder of IBM, had been pessimistic enough about the future of computers in 1943 to speculate that the world market for computers could not exceed five computers in the future.

TCS took shape in an environment where most people were unacquainted with computers. Even when they knew about the existence of computers, given the prevalent political sentiment of the time, they considered the machines a threat and did not believe in their capability to survive the test of time, let alone make an impact. So, if you were a bright, young lad born in the India of the 1970s and wished to pursue engineering, it was a given that you would opt for tried and tested heavy-weight courses like electrical or mechanical engineering and not take up 'weird'-sounding subjects like 'Electrical and Communication Engineering'! Computers then had the same status that artificial intelligence (AI) and the Internet of Things (IoT) enjoy today. The experience of one of the authors of this book at the start of his career is evidence of how novel computers were in those days.

ADDRESSING TALENT DEFICIT

The IITs did not even employ electronics, let alone computers, until the mid-1960s, even though the Nobel Prize in Physics was awarded jointly to William Bradford Shockley, John Bardeen and Walter Houser Brattain 'for their researches on semiconductors and their discovery of the transistor effect' in 1956. Most IITs then only offered electrical engineering, with a further categorization into light current and heavy current. While the 'heavy current' branch, which referred to power stations, hydroelectric power, etc. was the 'heavy-weight' category; the 'light current' branch referred to tape recorders, microphones and the like. IIT Kharagpur was the first to set up a Department of Electrical Communications Engineering in 1964.

Reminiscing about the India of those days, Gopalakrishnan says, 'I was one of the "brave" 25 who chose computers as a subject when I joined IIT Kharagpur in 1964. This was against the 100-125 participants who had chosen the rocksteady mechanical engineering branch. In fact, I suspect, these guys pitied us, in the belief that we had chosen computer engineering because we could not manage any other stream at IIT. None of us who chose this new stream were clear whether we would be hired at all, leave alone where we would get jobs.

'In the final semester, we had to write a thesis project. I was one of the handful of students who chose to write on computers. My thesis was titled 'How to design a 2-bit shift register.' I joined NELCO for my internship and later the Atomic Energy Establishment at Trombay for another internship. The atmosphere in both of these places just did not appeal to me. I wanted to be in an office atmosphere, wearing smart clothes. I felt confused.

'Some of my classmates had applied at IBM for a sales role. The Indian Air Force was another option for those desirous of pursuing a career in computers. But I was rejected. My poor vision led to the nation losing a good air force officer!

'In 1968-69, there were only three organizations in India which possessed computers—ORG at Baroda, Tata Steel and TIFR, Mumbai. In 1967, I applied to Hindustan Unilever Ltd. (then HLL) in response to an advertisement for engineering graduates and was selected. I was in the "Management Services Group". In my four years in this role, I found that the receptivity to computers was zero. The job appealed to me, but I would try to impress on my bosses the ways in which I could improve efficiency through the use of computers. In fact, much of my early years on the job were spent on trying to convince them that I could give them the desired information two whole days earlier than I could at present. However, they were unimpressed. "How does it make a difference if you provide the information two days late?" they would ask. However, in a move to keep up with the times, HLL ordered the IBM mainframe computer systems 360 and 30 in 1969. The latter model, 30, was faster than the 360 model. Launched in 1964, the model 30 could perform up to 34,500 instructions per second with memory ranging from 8 to 64 KB.

'I was sent to Administrative Staff College of India (ASCI), Hyderabad, to be trained in a computer-based MIS programme in order to work with the newly ordered computers. However, IBM's competitor ICL convinced my bosses at HLL that ICL-1903 was a better machine, and so the order was changed. I was now sent to ICL for training. However, this order, too, was cancelled later. This tryst with computers soon came to an end, as the Management Services Group was wound up and I was re-assigned to the sales and marketing department of HLL to sell soap and detergent instead. Hurt as I was, this felt like a sci-fi experience. My family had humoured me in my experiments with computers. The only person who was mighty pleased with the situation thus far was my grandmother, who saw my job—which involved sitting in an AC room throughout the day—as symbolic of having arrived in the world. Those days, it was a rare human who had the privilege of sitting in an air-conditioned room. My father himself had to remain content with a ceiling fan. "*peran AC room le ukararan* (My grandson sits in an AC room)," my grandmother would report with glee.

'In the meantime, well-meaning friends advised me to approach one F.C. Kohli in TCS, who, although a tough boss, was the only one who could help me realize my dream of a career in computers. Much as the dream of computers beckoned me, I decided to stick to HLL at the time, as I felt

I had a better understanding of the business, having spent some time in the company. My experiment with computers thus ended at an early age in my life!'

Evidently, the talent present in India had neither the incentive nor the institutional support to access the new industry—nay, world. This had obvious ramifications for skill-building in the IT industry. The Indian IT industry as we know it today could not have survived without strong institutional support to develop talent. Shapers like Kohli and Ramadorai played a crucial role in the development of this industry by building and nurturing IT talent.

Kohli could smell the future. Speaking on the talent scenario in India, he said, 'They (the politicians of the time) were not able to imagine what would happen 30-40 years later. However, in various science experiments, you need to be able to see the future. This country has more bright people than any other in the world. There is no doubt about it. But they get lost in the system. Few people realize that they are highly talented. The system does not know how to utilize them.' Whereas the political masters had no belief in computers given the large labour force in India, Kohli's conviction was that local skills had to be developed.

Kohli set the ball rolling by being actively associated with education right from the early years. Following an introduction to Dr P.K. Kelkar in the 1950s, who was then the principal of the Veermata Jijabai Technological Institute (VJTI) in Mumbai, he designed a course on control engineering which was introduced for the first time in India at VJTI. He would also deliver some lectures at the institute in his time-off from Tata Electric. Kohli then worked in close association with Kelkar when the latter was made responsible for establishing IITs in India, first in Mumbai and then in Kanpur. In fact, during his visits abroad for TCS work, he would do some talent scouting and faculty recruitment for the IITs as well. This led to IIT Kanpur developing the first M.Tech programme in computer science in India.

Kohli not only recruited many of the IIT graduates into TCS, but also invited several IIT professors to carry out training and consulting assignments there. Professors like P.N. Murthy from IIT Madras (now IIT Chennai) were tasked with helping TCS run specialized courses for people Kohli selected straight from college; all that these young students required was the aptitude, while knowledge of the relevant technology was provided by the IIT professors and other professional consultants. Kohli thus built a team with no past experience in computers.

His professional integrity may be gauged from his actions, as he never approached people from other companies for recruitment—what we call 'poaching' today. Of course, if people from other companies approached him for a job, they would be given a fair chance—but there was no active drive to hire from other companies. As Kohli says passionately, 'I didn't poach even when IBM left the country in 1977. I had a strong connect with the IITs—first with IIT Delhi and IIT Kanpur and then with the others. I built my own team.'

Kohli was instrumental in attracting the very best to the industry itself, as much as to TCS. The initial TCS team was comprised of bright young minds from the IITs, or graduates who had returned to India from US universities like MIT, UCLA and Harvard. When Ram joined the company in

1972, almost all the recruits were in the age group of 26 to 35 except for Kohli and Yash Sahni, who were somewhat older.

When Ram took over from Kohli, the realities of India had changed. IT and computer science had become the most desired courses in the IITs. Moreover, a significant number of computer science graduates preferred to go abroad right after their graduation, contributing to the 'brain drain' from India. At the same time, the IT industry was growing at a scorching pace of 40 per cent annually. Ram knew that while the culture of strong academic association built by Kohli, his mentor and ex-boss, had to be continued, the task of talent acquisition and management required a strategic rethink.

Ram, together with his TCS think-tank, deliberated on the way forward and concluded that the IT industry could no longer be seen as the sole preserve of engineers. Says Ram: 'There were three sources for talent acquisition. We would go to the campuses personally for recruitment. Then, we sent the senior managers to the alumni institutions they belonged to. We were never shy of recruiting people when we saw good ones without having any particular slot for them—essentially to build slack into the system. We have never been shy of bringing in the people, bringing in the technology earlier. Similarly, the people, processes and technology were always ahead of what we wanted to do. That is the mantra we have even today.'

Ram and his think tank believed that the criteria for entry had to be broadened to include the basic skills of logic, cognition and reason, coupled with high interest levels and a propensity to learn. With the right training, these criteria could be satisfied equally well by people with basic degrees in science and math. And thus was born the 'Ignite' initiative at TCS, for training non-engineering graduates to suit the needs of the IT industry.

The Ignite initiative under Ramadorai was a Shaper action of a similar stature to that of developing the IITs and consultants during Kohli's time. It possessed similar disruptive and multi-dimensional impact. It not only solved the short-term skills problem for TCS, but also provided beneficial outcomes and generated externalities on a scale that paved the way for long-term sustainability of the IT industry itself. From the point of view of a labour-rich nation like India, this move to train graduates from non-engineering disciplines gave birth to a new career option, especially for the traditionally under-privileged and under-represented segments such as women and those from poor, rural communities. TCS training became a great leveller!

INSTITUTIONALIZING LIFE-LONG LEARNING

Talent acquisition was important for developing leaders for posterity; but even more vital was nurturing such talent and retaining it. Leaders like Kohli underscored the value of life-long learning by creating a learning environment. To start with, this involved establishing a large library—in fact, the largest in India. TCSers would be encouraged to visit the library, given the company's operations in a knowledge-intensive business. Kohli would personally look at the time-sheets, which detailed the time employees spent on work and learning activities. He would insist on discussing the time spent by the employees in the library and even the books they had read.

Ram, too, swears by this practice of life-long learning. 'I strongly believe that in this business, learning must be a way of life at all stages of one's career,' he says. Such learning was accentuated through the practice of sharing such knowledge. As Ram says, 'When I read something interesting, I would send a note to Chandra (N. Chandrasekaran) or if we read something, say competitor information, we would write a note about it and share it. That is a habit. Keeping notes is always helpful in a number of situations. Recall and institutional memory is important. For example, TCS could have been folded up with Tata-Burroughs, but notes helped us state why we wanted to be what we are. In fact, today I scan such notes and keep them in a folder. Reading as a habit continues with most TCSers even today.'

Cultivating such a learning environment and Institutionalizing it was a must, even as the organization grew by leaps and bounds in response to new opportunities. Ram realized that while different TCS branches recruited people with specific skills based on their requirements, the new recruits would need to go through a centralized induction programme to ensure standardization and integration. In 1993, TCS set up a corporate training facility at Thiruvananthapuram TechnoPark—the largest IT park in India, set up by the state government of Kerala in 1990—and the first Induction Training Programme for its first batch of recruits commenced in 1997. In 1998, TCS commissioned its own Corporate Learning Centre—the Bodhi Park—with a capacity of 700.

In 2003, TCS shifted emphasis from training to learning, to account for the diversity in the learning styles of its new recruits, who were from varied backgrounds; the Induction Training Programme was rechristened the Initial Learning Programme. TCS has consistently utilized content developed by academic experts together with ideas from industry leaders to develop an appropriate curriculum. The curriculum itself is revised and adapted constantly to suit the changing business requirement. All new recruits go through the programme, wherein they are trained not only in software development but also in soft skills, cultural integration workshops, etc. over a period of 75 days.

TCS eventually set up new training centres in Ahmedabad, Guwahati and Chennai to help manage the increasing volume of new recruits. Then there was the Continuous Learning Programme for TCS' experienced professionals, and the Leadership Development Programme for potential leaders.

Ram also considers the process of close monitoring of projects and capturing the intelligence part of the Knowledge Management System at TCS. As he puts it, 'If a person is not put up for a project, the message is loud and clear that he or she has not performed and should be looking out for something else.'

WORKING PRIORITY: NATION FIRST, THEN INDUSTRY AND ORGANIZATION

The Shaper mindset is one that prioritises the organization over the personal, the industry over the organization and the nation above all. This is visible in Shaper behaviour and action. Kohli and Ram could both have stayed back in the West or even returned to the US after brief stints in India, especially in an era when brain-drain was well accepted. That they chose not to do so is a testimony to their desire to serve the nation and to put it above everything else.

Such a mindset is reflected in other behaviour as well. Harish Mehta recalls the time when he had returned to India in 1977, at the age of 31, to assess possible career opportunities and had applied at three places: TCS, the Department of Electronics (DoE), in Delhi and the Electronics Corporation of India Ltd. (ECIL) in Hyderabad. Of the people he met in India during this time, whether it was Kohli in Mumbai or Dr Seshagiri at the DoE, Delhi, he says, 'They were die-hard believers of self-reliance.' He admits that he had heard a lot about Kohli being autocratic. However, when he met Kohli to explore the possibility of joining TCS, he got a different picture. The latter asked him what he did. Upon being told that he was a data manager and had worked with state-of-the-art computers back in the US, the next half hour was spent in Kohli trying to convince him to stay back in India and contribute to the nation. 'It was not about "If not TCS, don't join anyone else"; Kohli was clearly concerned only about my not leaving India to go back to the US for a job. The focus was on India. That really impressed me,' he reminisces, sitting in his office in Worli, Mumbai.

Mehta recalls another instance of how Kohli put the nation and industry first, above anything else. This was in the early 1980s, when Kohli headed the software wing of the Manufacturers Association of Information Technology (MAIT). Mehta was then trying to manufacture a computer in India and had applied to the Government of India for permission in 1985.

'We had convinced Digital (DEC) to manufacture the computers. But we had MAIT's hardware division throwing spanners in our proposal. For instance, local companies could make the metal boxes (the cabinets); in our case, due to regulatory restrictions, we had to import these cabinets. We asked the government to charge us the normal duty, and not the higher import duties. But MAIT wrote to the government asking why we should be given normal duties. The metal for the cabinet was not being manufactured locally. After one month of collecting the data, we found a Digital Metal manufacturer near the river Mississippi, who said, "Sure you can make this cabinet in your country, but you have to take this 500-ton press to India. But, you only want to make 50 computers; I make 50 in a day." We figured it would be 10 times more expensive to put up a metal press in India than to even manufacture the computers. But MAIT continued to make it difficult for us. That spoke to me about the power of such an association. Bureaucrats were also helpless against these screw-driver technology manufacturers, who were essentially assemblers.

'We then met Kohli, who was heading the software panel at MAIT. We told him this is what MAIT is doing. He was very upset. He took it up in the next committee meeting. Whatever showdown he must have had, MAIT stopped throwing spanners and we got the permission for our joint venture manufacture. He told us later that he had threatened MAIT that he would quit if they continued to disturb the work of Mehta's company.'

Thus, Kohli supported a genuine manufacturer even by going against the very panel that he was part of. As Mehta puts it, 'He was very clear—his focus was India.' This nation-centricity is visible even today. Talking to Kohli, when we asked him about attrition, Kohli said forcefully: 'If people want to leave, you bless them. That is how the industry grows. This nation needs 100 TCSs.'

TCS, first under Kohli and then under Ram, contributed to building the IT industry through membership in associations like the MAIT and NASSCOM.[29] Mehta talks about the founding of NASSCOM and the challenges in establishing it in the presence of a body like MAIT.

'To my mind, without TCS, NASSCOM was a nobody. Initially, Kohli hesitated in giving his blessings. But TCS represented 55-60 per cent of the industry. So we had to take him along. It took us about a year to convince him. He was perhaps testing how serious we were. But then, he agreed and said Dr Nirmal Jain would be the TCS representative on NASSCOM while he (Kohli) would continue to be on MAIT, as he would like to see the healthy growth of both the hardware and software industries. After Jain joined, NASSCOM took off very well. We got the approval for telecom pipes, we received the export benefits and helped to build a healthy ecosystem for the software industry.'

Mehta was elected the first chairman of NASSCOM. After Mehta and Dr N.R. Narayana Murthy (Founder,

---

[29]Phadnis, Shilpa, and Sujit John. 'Kris Gopalakrishnan's Itihaasa Creatively Tells the Story of Indian IT - Latest News: Gadgets Now.' *Gadgets Now*, 17 April 2016, https://www.gadgetsnow.com/tech-news/Kris-Gopalakrishnans-Itihaasa-creatively-tells-the-story-of-Indian-IT/articleshow/51867538.cms.

Infosys), NASSCOM wanted the industry to move forward on to a different plane. They approached Kohli, who agreed to become chairman. But there was a catch. The chairman had to be elected, and this had to be approved by the NASSCOM Executive Council. Mehta confesses he wasn't sure if Kohli would agree to this. But Kohli said, 'You guys have a process. I shall follow the process.' Later, Mehta recalls, the Indian software industry, with a view to getting international branding, wanted Kohli to join Asian-Oceanian Computing Industry Organization (ASOCIO)—the regional level association for the Asia-Pacific software industry—as the chairman. He agreed, even though, once again, it meant contesting for the post.

Kohli's chairmanship elevated the NASSCOM brand. He became the voice of the industry, uniting diverse stakeholder groups towards a common goal. Mehta recalls how the association learnt to put industry interests before petty individual interests, right from the early days.

'While those in software services wanted duties to be zero, as there would be no custom clearance hassles etc., other members—the software product companies—wanted high duties as protection. We had this major conflict. We debated this issue for more than six months, before we took it to the government. Then we considered, let us see what is good for India over the next 10 years. A scenario analysis led to the conclusion that software duties should be brought down to zero, as the products being imported were not the ones we were developing in India anyway. They were two different categories. A staggered reduction in duties was proposed to give ample time for existing software product manufacturers to change their business plans. After arriving at this consensus, NASSCOM went ahead and requested the government to reduce the import duties on software to zero.'

Despite his influence, Kohli was mindful never to compromise industry interests or stifle their ideas. Mehta recalls how Kohli, during his tenure as NASSCOM chairman, wanted to introduce content awards for the industry. Some of the members were wary. The industry was small, and while awards could motivate, they could also polarise the industry and prove counter-productive. Mehta had to handle the task of informing Kohli about this view of the other members. He jokingly suggested to Kohli that they could institute awards provided there be a cap on the number of awards TCS could receive—at three out of the 10 awards. Kohli immediately saw the danger in what he was proposing in his enthusiasm, and altogether dropped the idea of awards. NASSCOM does not have awards till this day!

Kohli's absence of ego and ability to see the big picture is, again, characteristic of Shapers. Mehta recalls another incident highlighting the inherent simplicity and lack of ego-centricity in Kohli, which appears to be at odds with his reputation of always getting his way. Kohli had been elected as the Chairman of the Board of Governors of the College of Engineering, Pune (CoEP). He wanted Mehta to join him. He wrote to the Technical Education Secretary saying that he wanted Mehta to come in as a Board Member. The Secretary wrote back asking for three names to choose from. So Kohli then reverted, much to the chagrin of the Education Secretary: 'Harish Mehta, Harish Mehta, Harish Mehta.' Mehta laughs, 'Only he could do that.'

Mehta recalls another incident: 'In another meeting, I saw the same person (Kohli) pleading with one of the Education Department bureaucrats for a measly sum of ₹11 crore. When the meeting was over, I was very upset and asked him: "Kohli Saheb, for the CEO of TCS, what is the need to plead for such a small amount? ₹11 crore is nothing." In response, Kohli asked me, "*mera naam kya hai* (What is my name)?" I replied, "Kohli." He persisted, "*mera naam kya hai* (What is my name)?" I again said, "F.C. Kohli." He repeated the same question for the third time when it dawned upon me, and I answered, "Faqir Chand." Then he asked, "*Faqir ka matlab kya hai?*[30] For non-profit work like that of COEP, I have no problem in becoming a Faqir."'

Thus, Kohli gave his 100 per cent to any organization that he chose to become a part of. This organization-centricity was again something common to both Kohli and Ramadorai. Ram narrates the incident of an ex-TCSer who was very fond of cricket and would miss work to exercise his passion. Kohli reprimanded him sharply, saying, 'I know you like working for TCS, but also love cricket. You will need to choose between TCS and TSC.' TSC, of course, stood for Tata Sports Club, and the TCSer was given a lesson in priorities that he was not likely to forget in a hurry.

Mahalingam attests to the organization-centricity of both Kohli and Ram. He states that both of them had only one interest. They wanted TCS to be a highly technology-oriented company. In 1987, Kohli decided to buy a big mainframe IBM 3090 and install it in Chennai. The cost of this mainframe

---

[30]The word 'Faqir' literally means a poor man, who has renounced all relations and possessions and taken a vow of poverty and *dharma*.

computer (including hardware, software and custom duties) was ₹10 crore. This was a large amount by any standard in those days. What made it an even more audacious purchase was that its value was greater than the gross block of all fixed assets in TCS at the time. When Mahalingam remarked that they were betting it all on one computer, Kohli responded quite calmly, 'Yes, I realize that. Now, it is our problem to go and get the business.' Both Kohli and Ram believed in providing access to the best technology.

Mahalingam recalls that when Ram went to the US as resident manager in 1979, he created completely new contacts at American Express, Producers' Cotton etc., which he converted into major assignments. He also developed major relationships at GE and other companies. However, these contacts were always shared with other TCS managers, making them TCS contacts rather than personal contacts.

In line with Kohli's vision, Ram also believed in getting on board technically advanced organizations. One such organization was IBM Labs, with which Ram set up a relationship. Ram would shoot down any scepticism regarding TCS' ability to handle high-end projects like the C-BAM, taken up during his tenure: 'We have the capability; we have the infrastructure; we are also willing to get the government to look at the benefits of providing high-speed network to help the software outsourcing industry.'

Mahalingam says, 'They lobbied for this (help for the software outsourcing industry). In the early days, it was the Department of Electronics (DoE) that was responsible for setting policies for import of computers. Their thought process was to convince the DoE.'

Ram's biggest contribution to TCS, according to Mahalingam, was getting large clients on-board and entrusting significant top-end work to TCS. IBM Labs was one such example. Getting GE to outsource its IT function to TCS in the 1990s was another turning point in servicing large clients. The GE account brought about a sea change in how TCS was perceived and was a game-changer. These were the building blocks left for Ram's successors to build upon.

By Ram's own admission, TCS is so steeped in his blood that one of the few things that gets him angry is when people criticize TCS. In fact, one of the only two occasions when his wife, Mala, saw him losing his temper was when someone he knew quite well spoke ill of TCS. It is almost as though he takes such criticism personally.

PRACTICING A CULTURE OF AUSTERITY

A Shaper is one who believes in frugality above all and shuns ostentation and extravagance of all sorts. While every organization incorporates strategic cost-cutting, especially in difficult business environments, a Shaper sees frugality as a way of life and not merely as a means of riding over a difficult patch.

The business environment in the 1960s and '70s was difficult, with a shortage of foreign exchange and abundance of labour. Frugality and rigour were forced upon businesses. Long before venture capitalists made their presence felt in India, the only venture capital that TCS received was from Tata Sons. Kohli was always mindful of the Tata contribution and his accountability to Tata Sons.

Ram speaks of the culture of frugality that was ingrained right from the start. He recalls the incident of a relatively new employee who decided to take a cab from his home in the suburbs to the TCS office in South Mumbai. This was probably an accepted norm in his previous organization. When he presented the bills to claim reimbursement, he was summoned by Kohli, who gently rebuked him and advised him to aspire for fitness by walking a part of the distance to the office every morning. By doing so, he wouldn't have to spend such a hefty amount on travel bills either.

Tulsi Jayakumar, the co-author of this book, also experienced Kohli's famed frugality when the authors went to interview him. She states: 'As we started the interview, an attendant laid out some tea and three biscuits each for Gopalakrishnan, Kohli and me. I chose not to have the Bourbon and other high-calorie biscuits. Kohli finished his tea and biscuits, and so did Gopalakrishnan. As I finished my interview and thanked him, he drew attention to the biscuits I had left untouched. "You must finish these biscuits. They are really nice," he said, almost chiding me for wasting food. I finished two of the biscuits under his stern gaze before I asked him whether I could have a picture with him, hoping he wouldn't notice the last one, which lay untouched on the plate. Kohli not only practiced frugality but inspired others too.'

As a field engineer in his initial years, Ram himself was responsible for hardware maintenance of the Burroughs computers in India. In this role, he would end up working with his own hands, using screwdrivers, pliers and even sticky tapes to fix the equipment and keep it running. The 'Do

It Yourself' (DIY) approach not only helped save precious foreign exchange, but also forced them to learn about software systems and supporting hardware. Ram continues to believe that rolling up your shirtsleeves is the best form of learning. He is a votary for the 'frugal innovation' that India is known for, and believes that it was probably the 'developing nation attitude' that was once responsible for Indians being extremely creative when it came to finding hardware solutions and replacement parts—which is at odds with the 'use and throw' approach of today's generation.

Another incident that bears mention here was narrated by Pendharkar, then TCS' Head of Global Marketing under Ram.[31] It was 1974 and the first Burroughs computers imported by TCS had arrived in three truckloads under government seal, awaiting a customs inspection. The next morning, just before the arrival of the customs officials, the team discovered that an over-enthusiastic electrician, in his eagerness to help, had already broken the seal and unpacked the computer. Showing an admirable talent for improvisation, Ram salvaged the sealing wires from the dustbin, wrapped up the boxes again with the wire, threaded the seals on to the end and bent the wire so that the boxes looked untampered. The fear was that customs officials would confiscate the equipment were they to find that the seals were broken. However, the inspection went off well and the customs officials were none the wiser, and TCS landed its first computer from Burroughs.

Inspired by Kohli and Ram, even the TCS team in the

---

[31]'Ram Drive,' *The Economist*, 21 August 2008, https://www.economist.com/business/2008/08/21/ram-drive. Jayant Pendharkar passed away in May 2019

US took frugality to the 'next' level when they were invited to meet their first client. The 'frugal' mindset had led to the purchase of oversized shirts, trousers and coats—probably from a sale—and the use of sticky tape to hold up a folded hem. The result was that when a hand was proffered by the client for a handshake, what came up to greet it was a coat sleeve with no hand at all—as the TCSer had bought himself an oversized coat, hoping to fit into it for years to come. Moreover, the walk through the snow to the meet up with the client had led to the tape coming undone for another TCSer, who had then developed a trailing trouser leg.

Mahalingam, too, speaks of this frugality that TCS culture was steeped in. Both Kohli and Ram were mindful of the fact that money should be spent carefully, not extravagantly. Frugality should not be confused with being cheap or 'penny-pinching'. He recalled: 'Despite the fact that we were small, we had our office in the (plushly located) Air India Building in South Mumbai. Our clients were well taken care of. The focus was on business.'

He also narrated an incident that highlights the thought process of a Shaper. 'In 1983, I had moved to Madras (now Chennai) as Kohli wanted me to move there and build a business for TCS. It was still early years. We were not flush with cash. I asked Kohli, "Can we own a building in Madras?" Kohli replied, "Do you want computers, or do you want a building?" He was very sure about where he wanted to spend his money.' In the early years, regardless of whether clients picked up travel bills or not, Kohli expected consultants to use the cheapest mode of transportation. Programmers, too, were expected to take trains and not flights.

Harish Menon, Ram's executive assistant from 1999 to 2003, mentions an incident reflective of the simplicity and frugality that characterized Ram. One evening, when they were at an official event in Mayfair Rooms, a banquet hall in Worli, Mumbai, Ram chose to skip the buffet dinner laid out. Instead, he asked Menon whether he cared to partake of some simple, wholesome home-cooked food. A drive to his home later, Ram changed into a simple South Indian *veshti* and the two shared a spartan meal of rice, sambhar, vegetables and curd. Ram washed his plate and put away the dishes after the meal. Menon realized that this ritual was a personal habit for his boss. Later, he learnt that since Ram's wife Mala was away, the servant had cooked dinner for him that evening, which he did not want to waste. Menon speaks of the lessons in simplicity, frugality and humility that he learnt that evening.

FOCUS ON PROCESS AND EXECUTION

First under Kohli and then under Ram, TCS inherited a culture where process was supreme and customer-focused execution was given utmost importance. This can be seen as an organizational culture, shaped by mindsets driven by process-orientation rather than result-orientation, giving prime importance to execution.

Kohli knew that if TCS did not deliver, customers would not be attracted, especially in foreign lands. As such, he believed that TCS could deliver consistency by focusing on systems and processes. TCS was able to showcase its process orientation and attention to detail in execution right from its first project in 1979, which it undertook in the US with the Institutional Group Information Corporation (IGIC)—a subsidiary of the Union Dime Service Corporation. TCS drew up a simple contract to formalize its relationship with IGIC, which contained a clause called the 'best endeavour clause'—promising that in case of a problem, TCS would do its best to fix it using all the resources at its disposal. IGIC, at the time, used Burroughs computers. When Burroughs started losing market share to IBM, TCS helped IGIC in converting its existing Burroughs software applications to work on IBM hardware. At one point, TCS had about 50 technicians helping IGIC in such conversion work. The concept of offshore/onshore working introduced at the time sought to take advantage of the time difference between Mumbai and New York and effectively provided IGIC a 24-hour-a-day operation. The TCS services provided were so efficient that the client never had any cause for complaint, even though there was much resentment within IGIC due to the loss of jobs. TCS then added marquee clients like American Express. The exports business overtook domestic sales by 1984 and by 1992–93, exports contributed more than 80 per cent of the revenues.

TCS' emphasis on execution took on a new colour in the mid to late-1980s. This period saw TCS establishing its expertise in delivery of quality offshore work. This involved moving from merely sending engineers overseas to work under the direction of client management, to undertaking and executing entire projects at client locations and offering complete IT solutions for its clients. TCS managed to bag prestigious projects such as the contract to computerize the

Swiss banking clearing house, Sega Intersettle (SIS), also known as SEGA. In fact, TCS won the project over the client's regular consultants, Arthur Andersen, based on its superior analysis of the company's requirements. The Settlement System was successfully executed in 1993 and handled 4.6 million transactions in the first year of its operations. This project established TCS' reputation for quality delivery of large mission-critical projects in the important financial services vertical. The Y2K project during Ram's tenure led to the emergence of scale and established TCS' global credibility. With scalability came the need for processes to set high-but-uniform quality standards globally. Excellence had to become a part of the organization's DNA across every process. The result was TCS' 'Experience Certainty' campaign.

TRANSPARENCY AND GOVERNANCE

A Shaper is responsible for creating and nurturing a culture of transparency and governance within the organization. Kohli and Ram were both known for the culture of performance within TCS. Kohli was known for coming down heavily on non-performers and not suffering fools.

The manner in which he chose his successor at TCS was a lesson in transparency and governance. At the time, there were two probable candidates to succeed Kohli— Ram and Dr Jain; both were equally capable and had their own strengths. Who would be chosen was anybody's guess. Kohli prepared a scoresheet of the strengths and weaknesses of both Ram and Jain. He then went through the scoresheet with each of them before he announced his choice of successor.

So what considerations went into this choice? We were intrigued, since Ram and Kohli were very different in their styles of functioning. In fact, Ram mentioned this difference in styles quite candidly in his interview. We realized that the kind of considerations that went into the choice were again those that placed the organization above all. Kohli understood the phase at which the organization was poised as well as the trajectory of growth TCS was likely to traverse, one that needed a person who was customer-oriented—a people's person. The choice of Ram, then, was based on this assessment of the needs of the organization at the time.

Kohli reminisces, 'I interviewed Ramadorai in the US. The idea was to get people who could think differently. I was not copying (my) personality, but copying my brain. I trained him. Again, succession planning cannot go on forever. You need to let go. People should not feel like you are interfering even after letting go.' Similarly, such considerations went into the choice of N. Chandrasekaran when it came to Ram appointing his own successor.

Ram speaks of the time after Kohli's retirement, when Kohli retained an office next to his own:

'When I took over from Kohli, the rule was very clear: I don't want to hear anything about Kohli. Similarly, I would get annoyed if you were to go and tell Kohli about me. These were the rules. When Kohli gave charge to me, I was running the show. When I was reporting to him, he was the boss. If someone comes and tells you things, you have to be very clear and not encourage such (behind-the-back) talk. You cannot be wishy-washy and hear something only when it suits you. If someone did this, he was given only one more chance.

Change the topic, let him know you are uncomfortable. Such things happen in an organization when people try to play one against the other. It is up to you to handle this. As the leader, you set the rules of the game.'

Clearly, these are certain characteristic features of a Shaper mindset that distinguish a leader from a Shaper. It is possible that the following list is not exhaustive, but an emphasis on developing and nurturing talent; putting the nation and organization above the individual; simplicity and frugality; focus on process-orientation and execution; and creating and nurturing a culture built on transparency and governance are what we believe characterize the Shapers. Such a mindset allows Shapers to mould simple, unassuming organizations into institutions.

Chapter 5

Institutionalizing Transformation

First comes thought; then organization of that thought
into ideas and plans; then transformation of those plans
into reality. The beginning, as you will observe, is in
your imagination.

—Napoleon Hill

TCS as an organization grew, phoenix-like, within an
environment characterized by turbulence. It withstood
challenges and grew slowly but steadily in the first phase,
shaped by a man with an indomitable spirit and a never-
say-die attitude. With the leadership transition in 1996, TCS
entered its second phase—that of rapid growth and upwards
scaling, of a magnitude few would have ever imagined.
Possessing a different leadership style yet demonstrating
the same power of rapid and enduring transformation, Ram
built on Kohli's legacy to lead TCS into an unrivalled position
globally.

A transformation from a $160 million company

employing about 8,000 employees to a $6 billion company employing more than 1,60,000 employees in a period of 13 years (1996-2009) is remarkable and unprecedented—especially when most organizations are unable to withstand the pressures of expansion on such a scale, usually imploding during such transformations. A paradoxical fact is that even as India underwent a change from a 'less-developed nation' to the 'fastest growing economy in the world', TCS built and consolidated its business, largely globally, emerging as a top global IT firm with reduction of its India market to a mere 5.8 per cent in the first quarter of fiscal year 2019.[32]

Also, it is remarkable that the journey of TCS during each Shaper's era was distinct and unique. Each of the Shapers built the institution in their own ways, leaving their undeniable stamp. And yet, if we were to characterize Shapers as a distinct species (or even sub-species), say *homo plastes* (Latin for Shaper), they would differ from the regular *homo sapiens* in their mindset, behaviour and actions in a manner that is capable of producing massive organizational transformation. The results of such transformational leadership styles are 'Institutions'—to be seen as a sub-set of the larger category of organizations, but possessing attributes that distinguish them from the latter. Thus 'institutions' are organizations that develop within themselves the capabilities to endure over time and act as benchmarks for their peers.

We posit therefore that Shapers do leave their indelible mark on the organizations they help shape. However,

---

[32]https://www.tcs.com/content/dam/tcs/investor-relations/financial-statements/2018-19/q1/Presentations/Q1%202018-19%20Fact%20Sheet.pdf

when does such Shaper behaviour or action transform an organization into an institution? This, we believe, happens when actions pertaining to people, processes and policies get institutionalized. They no longer remain the mere whims and fancies of the last influential leader—his or her swansong, so to speak—but become a common language for everyone who sees themselves as a part of the institution. Further, it may not be incorrect to posit that institutions, although shaped by people, become shapers of those who choose to work and be associated with them. Thus, Shapers create institutions and institutions shape the Shapers.

Here are some of the attributes of Shapers that have helped TCS weather many a storm and endure for over half a decade:

Institutionalizing Talent Development

Picture this! The year is 1978. Ten years into business, even as TCS is struggling to establish a completely new industry in India, acquiring talent and grooming them, a move by Tata Sons to enter into a formal JV with Burroughs—called Tata-Burroughs—to sell and maintain Burroughs equipment in India shakes the organization into an existential crisis. TCS chooses to strike out as a separate entity in an area that would not clash with the new JV's business and cannibalize it. A diktat from Minoo Modi further prompts the transfer of 25 of TCS' high potential people to the new JV, which represents everything aspirational for the rare talent in computers available in India at the time—thus making the task of talent acquisition even more difficult for TCS.

From this point in time, when TCS boldly strikes out

as an independent entity, to February 2019, when TCS was recognized as a Global Top Employer for the fourth consecutive year by the Top Employers Institute, the company has come a long way. In fact, TCS was the only company among the top 10 IT services brands to receive this global certification of 'top employer'.

The Shapers' method of creating an institution of such reputation involves institutionalizing the process of talent acquisition and development as well as a culture of employee engagement and, hence, talent retention.

Talent acquisition in the initial phase was led by Kohli, who established strong relationships with the IITs. However, as the business grew—especially in the second phase—the scaling up envisaged would have failed had talent acquisition and development not been institutionalized. This involved a multi-pronged strategy, from talent sourcing to development, and involved forging relationships with academic institutions and universities to create special courses and programmes, developing new sources for talent acquisition, expanding the talent catchment area into tier-2 and tier-3 Indian towns, and developing training programmes like Ignite to transform the recruits from freshers to consultants who can travel overseas and speak the one language of TCS. These strategies helped TCS to increase its employee strength 40 times over 23 years, from 10,000 employees in 1996 to 4,17,000 in 2019.

Building Linkages

The nascent TCS witnessed the leader Kohli's personal involvement in the process, forging relationships and nurturing talent pools (aka IITs) to develop courses and

teaching ability in a desert of IT talent. A research centre—
Tata Research Development and Design Centre (TRDDC)—
was also established in Pune in 1981, with the goal of applying
science and technology for the benefit of the Indian industry
and Indian people.

Ramadorai extended this eco-system by creating an
academic interface programme that allowed heads of
premier educational institutions to get together on an annual
basis and discuss and deliberate on issues which affected the
future of the industry—trends, curriculum modifications and
the like—as well as explore opportunities for collaboration.
He also encouraged the head of TRDDC, Professor Dr Mathai
Joseph, to develop relationships with universities such as
Stanford, Georgia Tech and several UK universities including
University of York and King's College London. The idea was
to undertake, through partnership, long-term research work
in areas that would be mutually beneficial. However, such
a model still relied on acquisition of talent from a small
number of IITs, with the task of such talent development and
acquisition restricted to one or a few key individuals.

New Sourcing Model

As the organization and its need for talent grew, it needed to
move towards a new sourcing model wherein the talent pool
could be enlarged and dependence on key individuals for such
talent development and acquisition could simultaneously be
mitigated. Strategically, TCS needed to expand its catchment
area for talent, while at the same time ensuring quality hires.
Talent needed to be democratized and institutionalized!

A large and growing pool of senior managers was

entrusted with the task of campus recruitment, using their own alumni status in premier institutes to draw talent. At the same time, the TCS think tank decided that the youth on college campuses in tier-2 and tier-3 cities with backgrounds in math or science, who were keen on getting stable jobs with certain pay and other emoluments, represented vast, untapped potential.

It was a big, fat, audacious goal—to transform lakhs of fresh graduates from the nooks and crannies of India into 'consultants.' It required recruiting *en masse*, putting these large numbers through one large churning machine, which could then churn out talent of a type that could go out and perform on a global stage as the world's best trained 'consultants'—as TCS' business was mainly focussed overseas (See Table 2: TCS' Growth By Market: 2005-2019).

Igniting change

A new institutional initiative called 'Ignite' was launched in 2006. Ignite was a training programme developed by a six-person team at TCS led by Dr Raman Srinivasan. Initially, the team travelled to nine states not known for producing too many IT professionals, to recruit candidates and place them in the inaugural Ignite course. Over time, in keeping with its vision of allowing the IT industry to go national and create wealth for an entire section of the population yet untouched by the IT revolution, TCS developed a new digitized selection process which facilitated talent sourcing. An open online platform was introduced that college students from diverse socio-economic, cultural and educational backgrounds could log onto at any time and enrol for a test based on their convenience. The platform posts free content for students to go through till such time as they are confident about taking the test. The test itself is administered in centres across the country, for which physical presence is required.

Over 60 per cent of the trainees recruited in the first batch of 2006 comprised people who represented first-generation graduates; 65 per cent of these first batch trainees were women and over 60 per cent came from tier-3 towns, rural areas and villages.

Training global consultants so that they speak one language and present a unified TCS culture was a challenge. A training programme comprising an equal proportion of technical skills and soft skills was devised and implemented; each participant was put through training based on their needs as assessed through a pre-induction screening assessment process. An ex-TCSer—an engineer who later went on to pursue an MBA programme—states 'If soft skills are found deficient, the participant's training is extended even by a month. There is great emphasis on soft skills.' TCS views soft skills or 'people skills' as critical for preparing the individual for a global organization. Such soft skills helped TCS build key competencies both at the individual and the organizational level, such as cross-cultural communication and diversity management—which were necessary for creating a sensitive and inclusive work environment and allowed cross-cultural teams present round the globe to collaborate and work together cohesively. As Ajoy Mukherjee, ex-vice president and global head–HR, states: 'We also consider soft skills as a key leadership trait. We have integrated soft skill development into all leadership development programmes

Table 2

TCS' GROWTH BY MARKET: 2005-2019

Geographical Region	FY05	FY06	FY07	FY08	FY09	FY10	FY11	FY12	FY13	FY14*	FY15	FY16	FY17	FY18	FY19
	Revenue Distribution by Geography —Old Classification									Revenue distribution by geography-new classification					
Americas	59.5%	59.0%	56.2%	54.8%	56.2%	57.5%	57.5%	56.4%	56.0%	55.3%	54.0%	55.2%	56.1%	53.7%	52.9%
North America		57.0%	52.3%	50.4%	51.5%	52.8%	53.9%	53.3%	52.7%	53.0%	51.9%	53.3%	54.0%	51.6%	51.0%
Latin America		2.0%	3.9%	4.4%	4.7%	4.7%	3.6%	3.1%	3.3%	2.3%	2.1%	1.9%	2.1%	2.1%	1.9%
Europe	23.2%	22.4%	28.5%	29.2%	29.5%	26.7%	24.8%	25.3%	26.6%	28.7%	28.3%	26.8%	25.4%	27.7%	29.5%
UK		15.5%	20.3%	19.9%	19.0%	16.2%	15.5%	15.2%	17.1%	17.5%	16.7%	15.8%	13.9%	14.3%	15.5%
Continental Europe		6.9%	8.2%	9.3%	10.5%	10.5%	9.3%	10.1%	9.5%	11.2%	11.6%	11.0%	11.5%	13.4%	14.0%
India	11.7%	12.5%	9.0%	9.1%	7.8%	8.7%	9.2%	8.6%	7.8%	6.7%	6.4%	6.2%	6.3%	6.4%	5.8%
Asia Pacific		4.1%	4.8%	5.2%	4.7%	5.2%	6.6%	7.6%	7.5%	7.2%	9.3%	9.5%	9.7%	9.7%	9.6%
MEA		1.9%	1.5%	1.7%	1.8%	1.9%	1.9%	2.1%	2.1%	2.1%	2.0%	2.3%	2.5%	2.5%	2.2%
Others	5.6%														
Total	100.0%	100.0%	100.0%	100.0%	100.0%	100.0%	100.0%	100.0%	100.0%	100.0%	100.0%	100.0%	100.0%	100.0%	100.0%

with emphasis on managing cross-cultural teams.'[33]

Another distinctive feature of the training programme was that rather than relying on traditional teacher-centric, rote learning that only tests the memory of the participant, the programme focuses on active participation and collaborative learning. There is also heavy reliance on technology; the latest learning technologies, like real time classroom response systems, personal growth monitors, intelligent software tutors, gaming technologies and creative communication workshops are utilized.

As Ram puts it, 'We said that coming from various parts of the country as they do, we must get them together, so that there is commonality of purpose from day one. Sensitization to the TCS culture was a critical requirement. When we started, this training programme ran for over 12 months, now it has been reduced to three months.'

The idea of such training was to create certainty in the talent sourcing as well as development. The campus-to-corporate training programme became an industry benchmark to facilitate a successful transition from 'student' to an 'IT professional'. Six centres for such training and development were set up in addition to the training centre at Thiruvananthapuram. TCS also runs such training and development in countries like US, China, Hungary, etc., where trainees are hired locally.

A replicable, scalable and cost-effective model of talent acquisition and development, Ignite facilitated TCS' cost

[33]Mukerjee, Ajoy. 'Experience Certainty: Q&A with Ajoy Mukherjee.' *People Matters*, 6 March 2019, https://www.peoplematters.in/article/expert-views/experience-certainty-180

leadership in the corporate training space.

Engaging Employees for Life

Kohli and Ram, between themselves, laid the groundwork for a distinctive culture[34] at TCS—one that put people above everything else. It started with building TCS as a family organization, where leaders knew all the team members and their extended families. Ramdorai states: 'TCS is a family-like organization. Kohli knew not just me, but also my family. Tarun (Ram's son) used to come to the tenth floor (of the office) and play as I would spend 18 hours working in the organization. My wife too would come to the work-place. I practiced the same culture of knowing my team's family and extended family intimately.'

On the small things needed to foster a culture of engagement, Ram responds,

> You have to be available for people when they want you. We had a system wherein we had to meet at least 10 people every day, whether it was for two minutes or fifteen minutes, depending on the nature of the conversation. There was nothing about work, nothing about doing an assessment, etc. The conversation revolved purely around getting to know a person and making them feel at home within an organization. We had introduced a system wherein between 10 a.m. to 2 p.m. or 2 p.m. to 4 p.m., people could go and chat

---

[34]Organizational culture can be defined as the pattern of shared values, beliefs and assumptions considered the appropriate way to think and act within an organization.

with anyone. There was no need to take a formal appointment. That was the culture we had developed.

If there was a death in the family, or an employee died, the family had to see that you are there. They have to see you as the leader. There has to be a system to look at things like insurance etc. The family cannot be expected to take care of these things during a period of grief. Attention to small details when it is required the most is most critical. You cannot afford to lose the moment. That is what we say at home too: when a child comes to you and wants to share his joy with you, if you say 'I have office work, I am busy,' then you have lost the moment.

Maitree

As the organization grew, it required institutionalization of employee engagement. The concept of *Maitree* (meaning friendship) was born, initiated by none other than Mala, Ram's wife. The idea was to help engage the TCS 'associates'— as TCS employees were known[35]—and their families in activities that would bring them closer together. Later, with a view to carrying forward the Tata tradition of enabling the community, the scope of *Maitree* was enhanced to include socially relevant activities and endeavours, which would unite people working together on the basis of their interests and hobbies. The ideas that *Maitree* built on were those of TCS employees, who thus owned these ideas—be it the idea

---

[35]The term 'associate' itself was meant to reflect and communicate the pride that the company experienced in being 'associated' with the individuals concerned and held them as important and superior as the company itself.

of an adventure club, a theatre circle, a yoga circle, a music and dance club or even a toastmasters' club for personality development.

Ram also speaks of the need for an institutional mechanism for mentoring, as a means of improving the mental well-being as well as engagement of employees: 'The need for counsellors and access to counsellors in any organization is an absolute must, more so today than in the past. Stress factors today are very different. In the past, when I carried out mentoring or received it, the size and scale were different. The presence of the extended family today for dealing with stress is not like it used to be in the past. Support systems of the type that used to exist in the past don't exist today. I believe organizations are not doing enough to deal with this issue today. HR people would call people as No. 23 etc. That still happens in some organizations, where people are known by their employee codes.'

Thus, when an organization as heavily dependent on talent as TCS grows, it needs to put in place institutional mechanisms to manage talent. In fact, talent management becomes strategic to the business goal. As Mukherjee puts it, 'People are our single-largest asset. In the last decade, we have focused on every HR process to enhance the TCS experience for employees and drive high satisfaction levels internally. We believe that a happy workforce creates happy customers. Today, excellence is not just an organizational or individual goal, but a part of the TCS DNA'[36].

---

[36]Mukerjee, Ajoy. 'Experience Certainty: Q&A with Ajoy Mukherjee.' *People Matters*, 6 March 2019, https://www.peoplematters.in/article/expert-views/experience-certainty-180

This excellence translates into a vibrant, enriching workplace and best-in-class retention rates at TCS, which are key competitive differentiators. As Milind Lakkad, global head of Human Resources at TCS, puts it, 'Customers value the lower attrition because it results in greater stability and fewer disruptions in our service delivery. Moreover, TCS account teams are better placed to retain the contextual knowledge gained over time, and use that to build differentiated solutions tailored to each customer's unique requirements.'[37]

Talent management is reflected in attrition rates at TCS, which are the lowest in the industry. Thus, the annual report for 2019 reported an attrition rate of 11.3 per cent for TCS, as opposed to Infosys' attrition rate at 20.4 per cent. The industry attrition rate in the last fiscal year has ranged between 17-22 per cent.

NURTURING INNOVATION AND LEARNING

An institution is also distinct in the kind of innovation and learning environment that it nurtures. Ram himself attributes the low levels of attrition to the culture of learning and innovation fostered at TCS.

'It is the feeling of belonging. You work on it through whatever methodology—of which one of the clear paths is that of learning. If the learning is not there or if a learning

---

[37]'TCS Hiring Strongest in 5 Years, Joining Letters Issued to 30,000 Freshers.' Https://www.livemint.com, *Livemint*, 9 July 2019, https://www.livemint.com/companies/news/tcs-hiring-strongest-in-5-years-joining-letters-issued-to-30-000-freshers-1562673917728.html.

environment is absent, then people will leave. I have had situations where people have left and come back saying that learning completely disappeared. I have seen people in Australia, New Zealand and other parts of the world, where we have a get-together of the alumni. The difference between what they know and what they should have known is so great that you wonder how to relate to these guys in the first place. Quite a few come back saying we have been wasting our time, a higher salary or compensation is not worth it. Learning is a very critical component.

An important requirement for fostering the culture of learning and innovation was for people to be provided with requisite opportunities and support systems, alongside the faith that they would not be reprimanded for failure. These also become enablers for people to stay. Such an environment of learning and innovation also keeps up the excitement in the projects people work on and the kind of roles they perform.

A reflection of such learning is the industry-academia interface that has been encouraged by TCS. Pankaj Ghemawat, professor at Harvard Business School, was invited on board to be part of the core 'huddle' group at TCS responsible for strategy and execution. As Ram states quite candidly, 'I knew that it would be easier to get others on board for a change in strategy, were it required, if it was backed by a Harvard consultant.' The tradition has continued till date, with the current board comprising academics like Clayton Christensen, professor of Business Administration at Harvard Business School.

PROCESS ORIENTATION

Much of the shaping of an institution has to do with process orientation at an institutional level—focusing on business processes rather than functional structure and hierarchy. Empirical research points to such process orientation (PO) comprising multiple dimensions[38] including design and documentation of business processes; management's commitment towards PO; the process owner's role; process performance measurement; a corporate culture in line with the process approach; application of continuous process improvement methodologies and a process-oriented organizational structure.

The restructuring of the functions of Human Resource (HR) and Finance under Ram was an important step in the design of business processes at TCS. These two critical functions were integrated into the operations of the company. S. Padmanabhan and Mahalingam, two TCSers with hands-on operations experience, were brought in to head these functions. TCS underwent a full revamp of processes within these two areas in ways that built efficiencies, prepared the organization for scaling up and were perceived as just and fair by employees. For instance, from a back-office administrative system whose main role was to manage self-appraisal forms and to ensure compliance with regulations, HR at TCS came to occupy a key role in the institutional transformation, focusing on five key areas: productivity

---

[38]Kohlbacher, Markus and Gruenwald, Stefan. (2011), 'Process Orientation: conceptualization and measurement,' *Business Process Management Journal*, Vol. 17 No. 2, pp. 267-283.

improvement, talent retention, talent acquisition, succession planning and leadership development, and finally scaling for future growth.[39]

Even as an organization is moving towards process orientation and improvement, there may be resistance to such change within the organization, which may ruin all chances of transformation. Management commitment at this stage becomes the all critical factor. Ram narrates an incident of resistance faced internally within TCS while implementing the research done by TRDDC, which could help improve performance. This resistance could be attributed to a status quo bias. The TRDDC research had been readily adopted by companies other than TCS, and had in fact been extremely successful in improving performance in these places— including cement companies (ACC), Hindustan Zinc, Hindustan Copper and other Tata Group companies. It was clear that TCS was losing out on a key resource strength, namely its internal research competence. Ram decided to intervene. If a TCS unit did not use the TRDDC technology, he mandated that they would need to 'explain' the reason to him. This was a daunting enough proposition to encourage people not to resist. The TCS unit in Delhi working on banking systems was one of the test cases in this context. When they were asked to explain to Ram their disinterest in using TRDDC software technology, the resistance to the technology abated and TCS was able to develop a cross-banking product called 'Mastercraft' from this collaboration, and sell it to clients from 2000 onwards.

---

[39]Ramadorai (2009), *The TCS Story*, p. 109.

The strengthening of the process orientation requires a corporate culture in line with the process approach, complete with a process owner role and process performance measurement. Ram cites the example of the Manpower Allocation Task Committee (MATC)—an important committee during his time, tasked with manpower planning, resource planning and allocation. Those identified as high potential managers would head the committee for a period of about two years in their primary role, in addition to their other duties:

'If a project came up and it required a certain set of skills, the project manager would come and discuss with you saying, these are the kind of skills we are looking for; as the custodians of the repository of knowledge in the organization, we (in MATC) had to map the person for the job. In certain cases, we might have to pull out people from an existing project if another project needed them more, and reallocate them. We then would have to convince the existing program manager or project manager to release the people chosen. If we saw any project that was going a little astray, we had to step in to say that this requires more strengthening etc. Thus, a project became the responsibility of the team, rather than that of just the individuals working on the project. Project failure, then, was a reflection on the institution and the key members in the project, rather than an individual. That culture was visible. So, each was supporting the other rather than pushing their own self forward.'

Another aspect of the business process was the rotation of people across projects. Ram says, 'I have performed the role of manpower allocation, resident manager, project manager etc. So, if you look at the career of 25-30 years, at least 10-15 years, the TCSer, would have gone through at least 10 such situations where his experience would have been at multiple levels.'

Process orientation also involved ensuring that each project had at least one quality champion. Every project manager in TCS was mandated to be a Six Sigma Black Belt,[40] and software testers were encouraged to complete the Certificate of Quality examination. These processes helped TCS build a culture of 'quality certification.'

As the organization moved towards process orientation, putting into place several initiatives such as Ultimatix—the TCS digital intranet (see chapter 3) and Knowmax—a knowledge management process that connected TCS with its suppliers, customers and partners, the ultimate test of the organization having accomplished process orientation was the JRD quality value (QV) award. The annual award, named after JRD Tata, recognizes a Tata Group company that has achieved the highest levels of quality—a Tata Business Excellence Model (TBEM) score exceeding 600. The TBEM matrix or criteria have been conceived to deliver strategic direction and drive business improvements in the Tata Group. The award thus reflects an organization's use of an integrated approach to enhance performance management, which results in delivery of ever-improving value to customers and

---

[40]Six Sigma (6σ) refers to a set of techniques and tools for process improvement introduced by American engineer Bill Smith while working at Motorola in 1980 and adopted by Jack Welch as central to his business strategy at General Electric (GE) in 1995. A six sigma process is one in which 99.99966% of all opportunities to produce some feature of a part are statistically expected to be free of defects.

stakeholders, contributing to organizational sustainability.

The award is presented on 29 July, the birth anniversary of JRD Tata, every year. In 2004, TCS, under Ram, decided to apply for the JRD QV and won it—becoming only the second company after Tata Steel to do so.

STRONG LEADERSHIP

TCS' business model, right from its initial years, has been unique. Leveraging India's superior capabilities and skills in computer science and engineering, TCS was able to establish a global business by marketing firstly India, and next its own service offerings. TCS' business model evolved from carrying out migration to maintenance to optimizing systems and finally to developing the system itself. Migration involves moving sophisticated tools running on one software platform to another software platform without any loss in functionality. The initial model depended on TCS associates sitting at client locations. At that stage, most of the projects accepted by TCS were not domain intensive, as that would have required TCS to have specialists sitting at client sites, leading to potential visa and other problems besides pushing up costs.

As India opened up in the 1990s, new opportunities for different business models emerged, and TCS was quick to take advantage. The introduction of the X25 data communications protocol helped do away with the need to exchange tapes containing software code across continents—which was both time-consuming and lacked efficiency, as even a small change in the code would involve further delays in the project. The PC-to-PC links that the protocol enabled allowed for data to be exchanged with clients in real time. TCS adopted this protocol and bagged a large and prestigious contract to set up a dedicated Offshore Development Centre (ODC) for GE at SEEPZ, Mumbai. This enabled TCS to move up the value chain from offshoring of migration projects to offshoring small developmental production support and maintenance work and then further to developing systems.

While the model was unique at the time of its inception, all Indian IT companies today have developed similar business models. Whether Infosys, TCS or Wipro—the value proposition is the same, and so are the cost structures and the revenue streams. In fact, it used to be a joke in the industry that if you take away the names and logos of the Indian IT companies, you cannot tell one from the other.[41]

What was it, then, that led to TCS emerging as an institution and a bellwether of the Indian IT industry? The reasons for this may be found in two factors—one is project execution, and the other is the quality of leadership. TCS has managed to achieve the highest standards of execution by replicating its main model, established in India, across countries, even as it continued to globalize.

Analysts believe that the difference between TCS and its closest rival, Infosys, cannot be explained in terms of a difference in technology. TCS has nothing, in terms of technology, that Infosys does not. TCS' scale of operation and execution is much larger; more importantly, TCS owes

---

[41]"TCS vs Infosys: How the IT Big Guns Will Fare.' *Forbes India*, 14 January 2014, http://www.forbesindia.com/article/investment-guide-2014/tcs-vs-infosys-how-the-it-big-guns-will-fare/36921/1.

its success to its smooth transitions in leadership, which was not the case for Infosys.

Thus, we can see that while an organization may pursue a unique business model to start with, a large part of its transformation has to do with a culture that allows for good succession planning and leadership development. Within TCS, the transition from Kohli to Ramadorai to Chandrasekaran to Rajesh Gopinathan was smooth and involved old hands who had been associated with the company for a long time. This was due to the presence of a strong second rung leadership that had been groomed to replace the top level at short notice, were the need to arise. In the case of Infosys, the transitions clearly reflected a dearth of internally groomed top-level talent and continued dependence on the founder.

IMPACT ON SOCIETY

The true parameter of the success of an institution is its impact on society and the value it creates. In this sense, TCS stands truly unparalleled. In a time when jobs are the number one concern, both within India and globally, TCS stands out by the sheer numbers that it employs. In addition to its global ranking among the top 10 IT firms, TCS has also been certified as the Number One Top Global Employer in four regions—North America, Europe, Asia Pacific, and the Middle East—and as a Top Employer in 29 individual countries. Today, TCS is ranked as the Number One Top Employer in 16 countries: Australia, Belgium, Canada, Ecuador, Germany, Hong Kong, India, Malaysia, Netherlands,

Saudi Arabia, Singapore, Sweden, Switzerland, United Arab Emirates (UAE), United Kingdom (UK), and the US.

TCS transformed itself into an institution by institutionalizing transformation. In doing so, it has created its own path to success—what we call the 'TCS Way.'

Chapter 6

The TCS Way

TCS has become the benchmark for any company that wishes to go global. With a business model that has earned for it global revenues with Indian cost structures, TCS represents an institution that has had remarkable impact on India and its reputation globally, as well as on millions of lives across the world.

We have put together some lessons for students and practitioners of business to learn from the Shapers of TCS, and from TCS itself. In doing so, we believe there are certain commonalities between what the two Shapers did for TCS, which can be categorized as the 'TCS Way'. The TCS Way of shaping institutions may be summarized into a 4P model—Purpose, People, Priorities and Processes.

PURPOSE FOR SUSTAINABLE TRANSFORMATION

The first P denotes having Purpose or a vision. While having a vision sounds cliché, the fact remains that an organization without a vision can go nowhere. The vision represents the tangible direction in which the organization wishes to move, within a given time frame. Yet, it goes beyond just setting quantitative targets, as in the case of business plans. The vision must enthuse a large body of stakeholders at the same time—customers, employees, suppliers, and of course, the shareholders. The vision may be that of an individual, a strong leader or that of a dominant (say management) group. Further, it has to have a qualitative element—be attainable, yet dreamy and aspirational. A simple vision, followed by a well-planned strategy, forms the basis for a sustainable transformation. It is important to realize that the plans follow the vision. A strategy, with blueprints, plans, clear targets, etc., means nothing if you don't know where you are going and why.

Kohli's vision for TCS was to take it global and build a computing industry for India. The team under Ram knew that while the first stage of building credibility had been achieved, TCS would have to build scale. While the company planned a transformation in 2003, having become a $1 billion company 35 years since its inception, the initial thought was to look at a goal of ₹2000 crore. To be clear, this wasn't a vision but just a limited target. Much brainstorming by the members of the huddle group resulted in an actual vision being laid out for the company: 'Top 10 by 2010'— to be ranked among the top 10 IT software and services companies globally by 2010.

Accordingly, the phase since 2004 has been about establishing leadership. On 23 April 2018, about 15 years since it attempted this significant transformation, TCS became one of the world's 100 most valuable firms by market valuation, with TCS' market capitalization breaching the $100 billion mark. This was about 2.5 times bigger than that of its nearest rival, Infosys,[42] at the time. TCS went on to become the top global employer among IT firms in 2019.

A visionary leader is one who carries hope with purpose.[43] Both Kohli and Ramadorai were Shapers who were eternally optimistic and believed in their vision of creating an Indian IT industry, whether in the country or overseas. Each Shaper we have studied faced a unique challenge or crisis. Kohli faced the threat of merging with Tata-Burroughs and losing its identity, while Ramadorai faced the Y2K crisis. Both looked at these crises not as hurdles, but as a means of envisaging new opportunity areas. The ambiguities of the changes they faced did not deter them, as they looked at such uncertainties as keys to opening new doors and new vistas. It is also important to define a set of core values that can help guide policies and processes in order to achieve the vision. TCS had core values such as frugality, transparency and encouragement of dissent to guide its achievement of its vision.

How you translate this vision into behaviour and actions that support transformation is the domain of the next P

---

[42]'TCS Becomes First Indian Company to Breach $100 Billion Market Capitalisation.' *The Times of India*, Business, 23 April 2018, https://timesofindia.indiatimes.com/business/india-business/tcs-becomes-first-indian-company-to-become-100-billion-company/articleshow/63876020.cms.

[43]Emily Dickinson, American poet: 'Hope is the thing with feathers. Carry it with you wherever you go'

PEOPLE WHO OWN THE VISION

Having a purpose that only remains with you as your vision alone is a sure-fire way to failure. You have to be able to recruit and enthuse a bunch of people who can share your vision and thus help you achieve it. Aligning people to a vision for transformation requires consistent communication, so that everyone is on the same page and able to work towards the goal.

In TCS, the vision of 'Top 10 by 2010' was broken down into four parameters—revenue, profitability, number of people and market capitalization. This was communicated through town-halls to large employee groups and each part of the organization picked what 'Top 10' meant for itself, fostering a strong sense of ownership. This ultimately led to TCS not only achieving the desired goal but moving ahead, outperforming its peers, and occupying the global position that it does today.

An organization is only as good as the people it employs. Both Kohli and Ram fostered a culture of investing in people and nurturing learning and innovation, which created economies benefitting the entire ecosystem. The culture at TCS, to this day, seeks to foster high employee engagement both at work and outside it, resulting in higher employee satisfaction and, in turn, lower attrition.

The transformation of an organization into an institution, while led by a visionary leader, requires the support of a powerful guiding group or linkages. Kohli and Ram both fostered such linkages, with industry bodies like the MAIT and NASSSCOM on one hand, and with leading Indian and global academic institutions on the other. Ram introduced a participative leadership style wherein all strategic decisions were discussed and deliberated on by members of the 'huddle group.' The vision, thus, was shared by members of a powerful guiding group and consequently had a greater chance of success.

Empowering people such that they try to achieve the goal without fear of failure and censure is critical for a people-centric organization rooting for transformation. Every person in the organization, including the person at the lowest rung, should know where he or she belongs in terms of the alignment to the overall organization. Again, communication—which involves listening without prejudice or bias—is important for a leader. In TCS, 'Experience Certainty' is as applicable to the front-end sales person as it is to the chauffeur responsible for driving the manager to work.

Planning succession carefully and well in advance in order to create a strong second line of leadership is equally important. Organizations fall apart largely due to lack of the realization that leaders are mortal and the consequent inability to cultivate a strong second line of leadership in-house that can take over at short notice were the need to arise. TCS represents an institution that has had a fairly successful track record of succession planning and building a strong second line of leadership. It has been able to overcome a critical barrier to the endurance of institutions.

PRIORITIES TO SEE THE BIG PICTURE

It is important to deal with yesterday's bushfire without losing sight of the long-term. Many a time, the short-term is daunting enough to force the organization to be in constant fire-fighting mode. A Shaper possesses the distinct trait of thinking for the short-term without losing focus of the long run. This was true for both Kohli and Ramadorai.

At the same time, it is important to see the big picture. What is good for the country and for the organization is good for you. Country first, industry next, then organization and individual interests last, should be the motto for all who aspire to be Shapers. Often enough, personal ambition and greed overtake every other consideration—with leaders thinking in silos.

Both Kohli and Ram were driven by larger interests than petty personal aggrandisement. They were concerned with creating an industry for a nation that needed to mobilize employment for its youth.

PROCESSES FOR RELIABILITY

A successful transformation requires adequate planning as well as paying attention to the execution, which should be based on a strong set of processes that can be transported across time and geographies and are agnostic to the people executing them. The processes should be simple and robust enough to let people get the sense of a 'win' even before one plans a long-term 'victory'.

The latter has, in fact, been the hallmark of TCS'

competitive advantage, according to several analysts. TCS has witnessed a systematic setting into place of a set of processes that have allowed this global organization, involving employees in different time zones and cultures, to deliver a homogenous experience. 'Nothing succeeds like success' is indeed the right maxim for TCS.

Epilogue

This book is the first in a series about business leaders who have shaped their businesses into institutions. The other five books will be published sequentially. This series is the outcome of a nine-month process of curiosity and serendipity among the faculty members of Bhavan's SP Jain Institute of Management and Research (SPJIMR). One of the prominent privileges of being part of an academic community is the opportunity to raise questions whose answers are not known. This happened at SPJIMR one morning, soon after the Holi festival of 2018.

Through 2016 and 2017, the new and enthusiastic Dean of SPJIMR, Dr Ranjan Banerjee, encouraged faculty members to prioritize their focus on two tasks that would ensure SPJIMR's preparedness for the future. While the first task was to improve on 'management thought leadership', the second was 'to develop a theory that can impact practice'. Conferences and faculty seminars were undertaken in pursuance of these twin goals during 2016–17. On one such occasion, the faculty discussion dwelt on the distinctive role of enterprise in the growth and development of the nation. For example, looking at the rise of the US during the nineteenth century, it was instructive to think about how great enterprises were born, shaped by visionary businessmen, and grew to become providers of infrastructure to the nation, creators of jobs for the growing population and harbingers of prosperity.

We raised questions: what is the role of a business enterprise in shaping a nation's destiny? Can business partner with government to promote the growth and development of a nation? Can two destinies run parallel, yet converge to determine the growth of a nation and its future?

Like the US, which went from being poor and struggling to one of the world's greatest nations, India, too, is a multicultural entrepôt society, democratic and neoliberal. In fact, reading about the politics and social tensions the US faced in early times, an Indian could well get the impression that the US was no different from the modern-day Indian heartland: Pennsylvania and Illinois could easily stand in for Bihar or Karnataka!

In India, too, the first stirrings of economic liberalization began in the 1980s, several decades after Independence, culminating in the epoch-making liberalization of 1991. Emerging from a macroeconomic crisis, India has since become ready for great businesses and the Shapers of those institutions. Modern and durable business institutions are a desperate need for India, and Shapers of such institutions will be called upon to play a pivotal role in the India of this new millennium.

ALL LEADERS ARE NOT SHAPERS

A question then arises as to whether there is any difference between 'Business Leaders'—competent business professionals who efficiently manage corporate operations—and 'Business Shapers' or those business professionals who change the trajectory of a business and its growth by shaping their company as an institution. This question sparked a lively debate among the Dean and the faculty.

It was felt that while Leaders are preoccupied with details and the short-term more than the long-term, Shapers simultaneously deal with the details and the big picture, both immediately as well as in the future. India needs great business Leaders, but the time has come for India to also nurture business Shapers, if national dreams for the economy are to fructify.

The debate among the faculty began as a harmless, indeed an aimless exercise. Opinions were diverse and divided. Naturally, this made for an interesting research project. The authors of this book were very much part of these intellectual jousting matches. But the atmosphere around the subject began to gather gravitas and momentum. It is well known that exchange of information and socialization are essential to fresh thinking. The aggregate behaviour among some of the faculty was like the behaviour of blue jays—British summer birds that twitter a lot and are thought to exchange information collaboratively, to their mutual advantage.[44]

After several months, the faculty had assembled research jottings and anecdotal information, and had developed

---

[44]*The Living Company*, Arie de Geuss, Nicholas Brealey, 1997, p. 161

minds full of voluble opinions. The hypothesis that 'Shapers' are indeed a distinct category from 'Leaders' seemed to have great merit. Shapers' mindsets, behaviours and actions are fairly distinct as compared to Leaders. Simplistically, a Shaper is a higher stage of evolution than a Leader.

We then started to profile Shapers and Leaders and the differences between them. We had no pretension to analytical rigour, though we dredged through the literature quite diligently. We pressed on with our collective experiences and views, picking upon and developing modal opinions for further study and development. A benefit of pursuing such opinions is that hypotheses could be stated and then subjected to analytical or anecdotal verification through interviews and data gathering.

A PROJECT COMES TOGETHER

By Diwali of 2018, the contours of a team effort started to take shape. Certain faculty members expressed great interest in studying the subject and writing about their findings. Through an inquiry and search methodology, the team identified certain business institutions and Shapers as possibly meeting the evolving criteria. The faculty group did not want to be judgmental, with pretensions of rigorous and analytical criteria, as is usually the case with a jury that selects leaders or awardees. So what did the faculty want to do?

They wanted to list a bunch of institutions and Shapers that would be credible in perception, inspirational to research, and instructive to write about. Any selected institution should resonate with the mission and values of

SPJIMR—of influencing practice and values-based growth. No institution would be deemed above scrutiny, nor perfect in its image. Nonetheless, an important consideration among the faculty was whether the institution was, by and large, above controversy in its ethics and dealings. That is how the idea of the SPJIMR Shapers Project took shape.

In the meantime, Rupa Publications had mooted the general idea of writing books about the business leaders of India. As a faculty group, we were more interested in the institutions and, within their context, the role of institutional Shapers, rather than in writing biographies or hagiographies. The faculty was keen to write balanced research and anecdote-based books about carefully selected Business Shapers of India. The research material produced in this manner could be used for executive development programmes and management pedagogy in the future.

At this intersection of academic researchers' passions and publishers' interests, the concept was born for a series of books to be published by Rupa Publications. A question then arose among the faculty about why such books may be interesting to write and publish. Who might the readers be?

Historians have written about societies and political commentators have written about orbit-changing ideas.[45] Scientific writers have eulogized exceptional innovations that have altered the ways of thinking about the frontiers of human knowledge. The proposed books by the SPJIMR faculty could, then, be focused on the world of Indian enterprise and business institution-building.

---

[45]*Incarnations: India in Fifty Lives*, Sunil Khilnani, Allen Lane, 2016 & *Makers of Modern India*, Ramchandra Guha, Penguin, 2010.

There are writings galore on business institutions and Shapers, principally from the Mecca of business and enterprise—the US.[46] However, the faculty felt that there is a paucity of writings on Indian business enterprises, especially those that played out around the time of India's liberalization. This modest effort might encourage more studies for gaining valuable insights into companies over the coming decades, as there is a similar paucity of well-researched writings on Indian management literature. The role of great business institutions and their Shapers is unquestionably essential and laudable for the future growth of India, and its international management positioning. Everywhere in the world—and India is no exception—society is sceptical about business. There surely are lessons to be learned from organizations that have traversed a different path and blazed a trail of hope.

BUSINESS KEY TO NATIONAL DEVELOPMENT

We are very optimistic about the role of business as a force for good in society and in India, and about the satisfaction young people can derive from a responsible career in business and enterprise.[47]

Looking outwards to other countries, we spent some time trying to understand how the US transformed by going through three broad phases.

The first phase was from Jefferson to Lincoln (1770s–1860s), a period of about 90 years. The newly independent republic

---

[46]*Giants of Enterprise*, Richard Tedlow, Harper Business, 2001 & *Collosus, Jack Beatty*, Broadway Books, 2001.
[47]*Doodles on Leadership*, R. Gopalakrishnan, Rupa Publications, 2019.

was learning to deploy democratic politics and institutions, and was largely fuelled by immigration, slaves and westward expansion.[48]

After Lincoln had effectively dealt with the divisive issue of slavery, for the next 60 years till the tenure of President Teddy Roosevelt (1860s till 1920s), there was a period of mostly unbridled capitalism—the era of the mafia, the great robber barons and the California gold rush.

Over the next century, from Roosevelt to modern times (1920s onwards), the US can be considered to be in the third phase, with the state having learned to control business for the larger good through laws, democracy, and justice systems. All these phases have played out over two-and-a-half centuries.

By contrast, India can and will achieve similar progress in less than half the time that the US took—may be from the 1990s until the end of the twenty-first century. Viewed in this manner, India is about a third of the way through; for sure, the best is yet to come. Throughout our work experiences, we have watched with fascination how old, inefficient jobs give way to new, more efficient processes. Societies and nations need the engines of powerful business and enterprise to create jobs, economic growth, and hope for aspirants.

SHAPER'S MINDSET-BEHAVIOUR-ACTION (MBA) GRID

This project is about discovering the distinctive approach of institutions' Shapers that sets them apart—the way they think

---

[48] *Team of Rivals*, Doris Kearns Goodwin, Simon and Schuster, 2005

and act. Careful deliberation on the differences between 'Leaders' and 'Shapers' led to a construct that we have named the Shapers' MBA Grid. The chart in the Appendix is a schematic representation of the idea. We visited the matrix as a reference point repeatedly as we narrated the stories of these institutions.

A related question arises: how much of the institution's success should be attributed to the leader personally? When companies succeed, very often, the leader gets the credit, as if he or she had fashioned it. When companies fail, the leader usually attributes the failure to external factors outside of his or her control. Views on how much of the credit or blame should be ascribed to the leader have varied for a long time, and occupied both ends of the possibilities.

The social philosopher Thucydides, writing even before Plato, described how Athenian leaders like Pericles played a crucial role in the Sacred Wars that led to democracy and the establishment of the Athenian empire; in this perspective, the leader did the heroic acts and deserved to be eulogized. Contrarily, Karl Marx argued that leaders operate in circumstances that they do not choose, so they 'do not make history as they please.' They are merely instruments of a set of existing circumstances and material conditions.[49]

To avoid this debate and intellectual trap, the authors have focused on learning from the progress of the institution rather than view the Shaper as the hero. Institutions are rare, and building them is not an easy task. It requires a Shaper with

---

[49]*The Eighteenth Brumaire of Louis Bonaparte*, Karl Marx, 1852

a distinctive mindset to design institutions. As we embarked on the mission of researching and writing on this subject, we realized that our work might seem to resemble a certain bestselling book from 1994.[50] We do not deny the potential influence of the thinking that led to the bestselling book of 1994, and acknowledge the likely influence of that work as well as many other books from which we have learnt, even if osmotically. After all, influencing thinking and practice is the fundamental motto of authors and writers. It also happens to be the aim of the thought leadership that Bhavan's SPJIMR wishes to advance. However, our approach is quite different from the 1994 book in five important ways.

First, it explores the subject from an Indian point of view, not a global or American perspective. The truth of the matter is that, for business, the context matters.

Second, each book, authored as it is by a combination of an accomplished practitioner and a distinguished academic, produces a different point of view.

Third, the focus of this series is on organizations that are Gen-L, in which the main actions occurred within the last half-century. The 1994 book was about well-established organizations, perhaps a century old at the time. Indeed, it was a criterion for the 1994 book to review succession planning and its efficacy. Our research included companies where the test of succession planning had not yet occurred.

Fourth, we have neither used significant analytics nor comparator companies to justify the inclusion of a Shaper institution. We avoided the 'mathiness approach', to borrow

---

[50]*Built to Last*, James Collins & Jerry Poras, Harper Business, 1994

a phrase from economist Paul Romer, and relied on the 'truthiness approach', advocated by television commentator Stephen Colbert.

Finally, we sought Indian organizations which were 'not inherited organizations' quite in contrast to the seminal work of 1994. We interviewed Shapers who were still on the task, not Shapers whose work had been done and recorded in history.

We sign off by noting that an entrepreneurial mindset is re-emerging in India. Unlike the earlier generations, young Indians are no longer obsessed with India's poverty, but with its future. This gives India a fighting chance. We would wish to make three points regarding entrepreneurship: first, that it has been in the national gene; second, that the openness to productivity ideas has been a strong driver and the embrace of the IT revolution adduces to that; and third, that entrepreneurship is contagious and success attracts others in a virtuous cycle, a cycle in which India is now happily placed as the third-largest start-up nation in the world. These facts further strengthen our belief that India needs not just companies, but also Shapers who have learnt how to build an institution.

Tata Consultancy Services is a great exemplar of all of the above.

Appendix

Research Methodology: Shaper's 'MBA' Grid

A section on research approach and methodology seems out of place in a practice-oriented book, which aims to guide the modern day manager and leader to be the Shaper of an organization that can outlive most of its peers and be hailed as an institution through its actions. While the book aims to be practitioner relevant—given the ambitious goal of studying six different organizations recognized as institutions in India and discerning patterns—the research project was guided by a theoretical construct, which was the result of serious deliberation and iteration. We termed this construct the **'Shaper's MBA Grid'**, which is an important contribution as it has the potential to act as a beacon for other researchers interested or working in the field of leadership and organizational behaviour in the Indian context.

As such, we decided to 'relegate' the research approach and methodology to an appendix section, rather than use a book chapter for the same. The advantage of an appendix is that it can be skipped by those disinterested in the research approach itself without much loss of continuity in narrative. At the same time, it seemed apt to present serious researchers—who seek to further the research agenda on the theory and practice of institution-building—with a thorough understanding of the mindset and action patterns of institution builders.

Again, unlike the conventional research methodology section in an academic paper, we shall seek to keep this section light, highlighting the 'What', 'Why' and 'How' of our research in language that will appeal to the lay reader as much as to the seasoned academic.

THE 'WHAT'

The Shapers Research Project owes its genesis to a serendipitous discussion amongst a few SPJIMR faculty members in 2018 on the distinction between organizations and institutions and the distinction between their leaders. Discussion veered around Indian companies that feature in the Fortune Global 2000 list. There were about 50, including those like Reliance Industries (in the top 200 list) and TCS (in the top 500 list). There was consensus—tentative at this stage—that not all these organizations were 'institutions'. Also, while these organizations are aspirational to several MBA students who seek to find jobs with them, they offer little hope to the sceptic who is convinced about the mortality of corporations.

An influential piece of research in 2012 by Professor Richard Foster from Yale University, for instance, posited that the average lifespan of a company listed in the S&P 500 index of leading US companies has decreased by more than 50 years in the last century—from 67 years in the 1920s to just 15 years today.[51] Another study found the timespan of business survival to be merely 10 years.[52]

Given that most Indian businesses have emerged post the opening up of the Indian economy in 1991 and yet face multiple business challenges in the current uncertain and volatile business environment, the question that emerged was: 'Which of these organizations will survive long enough? Which Indian businesses are institutions?'

At this stage, we defined the term 'institution' itself as an organization that had, at its core, certain universally accepted values and norms for which it was revered; an organization that had withstood the test of time—having been established within a decade or two since Independence—and seemed to possess an innate resilience to be able to withstand multiple business challenges, having already survived several such challenges in the last several decades.

As we began to identify some of the organizations that qualified as institutions, as well as the factors that distinguished them from others, a Eureka moment came in the realization that the phenomenon of institution-building is deeply linked to the leadership experience that each one goes through. In particular, we realized that the hypotheses for the research project, were it a conventional one, could very well read as follows:

---

[51]https://www.bbc.com/news/business-16611040
[52]https://fortune.com/2015/04/02/this-is-how-long-your-business-will-last-according-to-science/

H1: The number of years an organization survives is linked positively to leadership performance.

H2: The ability of an organization to withstand business volatility and severe business challenges is linked positively to leadership performance.

H3: The reputation that an organization carries is linked positively to leadership performance.

Needless to say, our preliminary research into institutions was guided by a literature review of scholarly work on institution-building, ranging from Powell, Arie de Geus, Di Maggio, Meyers and Rowan to Indian scholars like Udai Pareek.

This then led to the question: What sort of leadership performance will qualify for such transformation of ordinary organizations into venerated institutions? The obvious answer was 'Transformational' leadership of a sort that transcends the current notion of leadership, as enunciated by Goleman, Moss Kanter and others—a leadership that not only transforms, but rather 'shapes' the organization into an institution. Such leaders may be called 'Shapers.' We also realized that just as there are only a few organizations that may make it to a list of 'institutions,' there are only a few business leaders who may qualify as 'Shapers' of institutions.

This led us to an additional hypothesis:

H4: Leadership mindsets, behaviours and actions undertaken by 'Shapers' are unique and distinct from those of Leaders.

We thought we were on to something interesting with this discovery. The next obvious question was: could we—a group of interested researchers—work on a set of Indian organizations that *we* could identify as institutions, using a commonly accepted set of parameters? The set of such institutions need not be exhaustive. However, they need to conform to the parameters laid out, and should not be deemed questionable by the set of researchers working on the project, which now had a name—the SPJIMR SHAPERS PROJECT. Can such institution-building be studied in the context of the leaders, who, as Shapers, shaped and created them in a manner such that they have become enduring? Could we study and glean a set of uniform mindsets, behaviours and actions that would set these leaders apart from other leaders who are non-Shapers? And how do these Shapers shape their organizations into institutions?

This then leads to the second aspect of our research: why did we want to do this?

THE 'WHY'

Well, we could advance a large number of great-sounding explanations for why we undertook this research project—explanations such as: 'We wanted to understand the mindsets and actions of Shapers so that it can help create Shapers for the future.' Or, 'We want to make a difference to Indian management discipline and practice.'

These reasons are valid and good reasons to conduct any such research. However, as every well-intentioned researcher in the field of social science will testify: we undertake research when the theme excites us. It helps us uncover phenomenon of which we have little understanding but wish to unravel for ourselves. In the process, we do help set the research agenda for others as well.

In this case, it made sense, as we could discern hints of a pattern emerging even as we began to do our preliminary research based on secondary data. We realized that rather than talking about leadership types in an anecdotal fashion, we could possibly decipher a method to such transformational leadership—not consciously agreed upon by those who practise it, but present all the same, waiting to be discovered and possibly even replicated.

In particular, what excited us were questions like:

▸ How does one distinguish an institution from an organization, even if the key metrics used to map organizational performance are similar—that is, involve deeper qualitative questions than merely looking at quantitative metrics? Thus, for instance, why should Reliance not feature in our list, even though it is one of the top Indian companies on the Fortune Global 2000 list?

▸ What transforms an organization into an institution? (The emphasis was on the process and not the outcomes.)

▸ What mindsets, behaviours and actions set a Shaper apart from a leader? This would entail a deep qualitative analysis, which could form the basis for a new theoretical construct, called the 'Shaper' construct.

▸ How and when does a leader qualify as a Shaper?

These questions also became the 'Why' or the 'purpose' of our research. In the process, if we are able to expedite the transformation of some business organizations into institutions through their leaders adopting the right 'Shaper' mindset, that will be a happy, albeit unintentional, consequence of this book and project.

This leads us to our final question: How did we manage to undertake and bring to fruition this project?

THE 'HOW'

The process of short-listing the tentative candidate organizations for the research project was undertaken by a small group, comprising the authors—including the lead author, R. Gopalakrishnan—and Ranjan Banerjee, the Dean of SPJIMR. A set of six institutions were initially shortlisted, with the understanding that a second round of other institutions could be worked on at a later stage. The institutions shortlisted in the first round included, in alphabetical order: Biocon, HDFC, Kotak, L&T, Marico and TCS. The methodology we sought to use in the project was a case study approach, involving in-depth interviews and triangulation. The project was then presented to the publisher, and approval was sought.

Each of the co-authors, well-respected academics in their own right, began with carrying out background research on their subject of study—both the Shaper and the institution. In the case of this book on TCS, we researched two Shapers for the same institution.

We deliberated, discussed, and arrived at the idea of a 'framework' that could be used to explore the main hypotheses. This was named the SPJIMR MBA Grid. The contents of the grid itself were arrived at through an iterative process of refinement as the research progressed.

In the initial stage, the grid was visualized as a 9*9 matrix with Managers, Leaders and Shapers as distinct agents along task and process dimensions. The task dimensions considered were: Managing the Core, Preparing the Future and Creating the Future. Along the process dimension, Managers were hypothesised as focusing on Policies and Processes; Leaders as focusing on Performance, while Shapers would focus on People. Juxtaposing the task and process dimensions, we arrived at a set of nine unique actions, which would set apart Shapers from Leaders and Managers.

In Stage 2, we refined this further to arrive at an 8*3 matrix. The vertical dimension (the columns) looked at Mindset, Behaviour and Actions, while the horizontal dimension (the rows) looked at the MBA categories broadly based on the 4Ps: Purpose, People, Policies and Processes. A Shaper was identified in terms of his or her mindset along eight dimensions: People Relations, Short-term and Long-term Focus, Critical Thinking, Orbit Shifting, Breaking Barriers, Levers of Change, Cyclical Learning and Stakeholder Orientation. We reproduce the MBA grid below.

The next step was to seek in-depth interviews with the 'Shapers' of these institutions, as also with multiple stakeholders, who could shed light on various dimensions of the Shaper in question and their institution. While we decided and planned for the interviews, the idea was clear: these books were not meant to be hagiographies. While there were protagonists within the case study approach who were the Shapers, the 'heroes' were clearly the institutions, which had withstood the test of time and made distinct contributions to nation-building. Again, it was a conscious decision not to attempt to discuss the warts et al. of the Shapers, the reason being that we are interested in understanding the positive mindset that contributes to the building of a Shaper—an individual who, despite largely having an unblemished track record, is nevertheless as human as any of us in terms of frailties and vulnerabilities. Nowhere, then, should the book be construed as an attempt to idolize a human being with a larger-than-life image.

Each researcher conducted at least three such interviews with different people associated with the Shaper and/or the institution in question. Some of us met our protagonists more than once as well. The questions used to test the hypotheses included some generic questions, as also others that were specific to the particular institution or Shaper. They included questions which revolved around institution-building, such as:

- How did you set the organizational vision, values and performance expectations?
- How do you attract, retain and enhance talent within your organization?
- What is the purpose of the leadership? How do you communicate with your workforce?
- How do you arrive at and institutionalize the core values of the organization?
- What is the role of 'out-of-the-box' thinking and an entrepreneurial mindset for any organization? How do you ensure that such a mindset gets internalized into the DNA of the institution?

- How do you and your senior leadership team guide and sustain the organization?
- How do you develop future leaders, measure organizational performance and create an environment that encourages ethical behaviour and high performance?
- What are the institution's core competencies, work systems and designs that help to create value for your customers?
- How do you identify the organization's blind spots in achieving long-term organizational success and sustainability?
- What specific processes in institution-building have you undertaken?
- How have you addressed succession planning in your organization?

There were other questions pertaining to each Shaper, which sought to explore key facets of their life that helped 'shape' the Shaper, starting from childhood, as well as their role models etc. Another interesting question posed to the Shapers was: if they were given another three to five more years at the helm, what would be the key 'unfinished' agenda that they would want to address?

All these questions helped glean the Shaper's mindset, behaviour and actions relating to specific aspects of institution-building. We probed three specific areas: Building the institution (sometimes from scratch), seeing it through troubled times and changing the course. The idea was threefold: Understanding the context, understanding the leader and understanding the institution.

The book chapters have also been aligned accordingly. The initial chapters set the context in which the organization developed, while the next set of chapters look at the life and key influences on the Shaper, as also specific aspects of the Shaper's mindset, behaviour and actions. The last set of chapters cover the institution—what makes it qualify as one, the salient features of an institution and understanding the future of the institution.

SPJIMR SHAPER'S MINDSET-BEHAVIOUR-ACTION GRID

Mind set	Behaviour	Action
People relations: Respectful to others	Sensitive and empathetic to others	Engages with people and nurtures them
Short-term vs long-term: Both are equally important	Encourages to deal with the immediate, while silently considering the long-term	Acts on the immediate decisively to get results, creating the impression of small wins, so as to look forward to and work towards a big 'victory' in the future
Critical thinking: Considers options and their pros/cons in mental evaluation	Encourages discussion and debate with open-mindedness	Acts with precision and demands accountability
Orbit changing: Constant evaluation of which orbit change will benefit the organization	Tosses around and debates the risks and rewards of orbit change, almost appearing indecisive	Demonstrates single-minded commitment once a decision is made

Break barriers: **I have the freedom** **to act if I am** **willing to steer** **through obstacles**	Identifies the obstacles and seeks the best way to deal with them—break them, go around them, navigate them	Once the path is clear, pursues with an Arjuna-like determination
Levers of change: **Action is within** **my reach:** **must change** **complacency to** **the aspirational** **mindset**	Debates and seeks ways to dislodge the organization from negative hooks while attaching positive hooks	Presses for action and change in a disciplined manner
Cyclical learning: **Action Observation** **Benchmark** **Review-Act again**	Insists on a systems approach of cyclical learning	Ensures organization-wide deployment of an accepted system
Stakeholder **orientation:** **What is good for** **the stakeholder** **is good for the** **institution and** **hence, for us**	Constantly understanding customer and community perspective	Always acts by keeping in mind multiple stakeholder interests

Acknowledgements

Although this section is placed at the end of the book, it in no way takes away from the role that family, friends, colleagues and others have played in the shaping of this project. In fact, but for such support, this book would never have been.

We thank the publishers, Rupa Publications, who reposed confidence in a book series of this sort. The Rupa team—especially Yamini Chowdhury, who worked with the six Shapers of this book patiently—deserves special mention.

We thank the Shapers—F.C. Kohli and S. Ramadorai— who spared their time to speak with us and narrate anecdotes and life experiences that have found their way into the book. The staff in their offices, Shital Palnitkar and Sapna Hemant respectively, who ensured that schedules were matched so that the book could be completed within time. Others who helped provide information for this book include Harish Mehta, S. Mahalingam and Syamal Gupta, who gave us deeper insights into the context in which TCS was shaped and how the 'Shapers' have achieved the legitimate place accorded to them by this series.

We are also indebted to Mr Arun Gandhi, former director, Tata Sons, for reviewing the manuscript painstakingly and making comments that forced us to clarify certain concepts and edit sharply in order to prevent any duplication of content.

This book owes its origin largely to the environment of discussion and debate encouraged and fostered by Dean Ranjan Banerjee. He envisaged this project as one that would advance 'Thought Leadership' in the field of management education. It is because of him that the collegiate atmosphere at SPJIMR, as also getting eminent management practitioners on board, materialized. One of them eventually became the lead author of this book series. Such collegiality also ensured that the six different faculty members associated with the Shapers book series have been able to write six different books, and yet leave you in no doubt that they have been drawn from the same stock. The theme itself resonated with most of the members involved in this book series, as it was one that even the previous Dean, Dr Manesh Shrikant, had been passionate about and sought to research. We feel privileged to be working on a dream we have seen long in the making.

Tulsi thanks all the fellow authors of the other books in the series (in alphabetical order)—Anant Narayan, Lata Vidyut Dhir, M.S. Rao, Pallavi Mody and Sushmita Srivastava. It was reassuring and comforting to hear of similar trials and tribulations during the process of writing, while at the same time being able to bounce ideas off each other. Do's and don'ts were meticulously shared on the WhatsApp group created for the purpose. She also wishes to thank the library staff at SPJIMR—Mallappa Kumbar and Sanjay Narvekar, who have always helped retrieve any literature that we wanted for reference purposes. She also thanks members of her administrative team at the Family Managed Business programme, who have always supported her need to manage research and academic work.

And finally, we owe a debt of gratitude to our families: Geeta, Gopalakrishnan's wife; and Jay and Radhika, Tulsi's husband and daughter respectively, who have provided emotional support at all times and have kept up the faith.

Gopalakrishnan and Tulsi

Index

Los Angeles (UCLA), 37, 38, 65

ULTIMATIX, 46

Viswanathan, Paigal S., 43, 46

Viswanathan, Ravi, 43

Veermata Jijabai

Technological Institute (VJTI), 64

Alfa Laval, 25, 26

Y2K, 35, 42, 43, 44, 45, 47, 83, 110